# DESIRE

*the*
EMOTIONAL
APPETITE
*for*
SUCCESS

## MELVIN MURPHY

© 1995 Melvin Murphy
P.O. Box 2868
Merrifield, VA 22116

LCCN 95-94334
ISBN 0-9646799-0-6

Cover & Graphic Design:
**Don Starr / Starr Design**

Cover Photograph:
**Edu. Bernardino**

All rights reserved. No part of this publication may be reproduced, stored in a retrieval system, or transmitted, in any form, or by any means electronic, mechanical, photocopying, recording or otherwise, without the prior written permission of the copyright owner.

---

Printed in the USA by

Morris Publishing

3212 E. Hwy 30
Kearney, NE 68847
800-650-7888

*To Linda,
Always follow
your Desires,
[signature]*

## DEDICATED TO:

**Christian Daubert.**
*Thanks for being my best friend
and helping me grow.*

**My siblings Desiree, Michael, William and Juan.**
*I finally broke the circle.*

**My mom and dad William C. and Vernell Murphy.**
*Thanks for the guidance during my childhood.*

**My aunt Cathy W. Moore.**
*May your desires for spiritual wealth be given to you.*

**My late granddad James B. Williams.**
*I kept my promise.*

# ACKNOWLEDGMENTS

There are so many people—too many to name who inspired me to write this book—I want to give a special thanks to.

Thank you, my good friend **Vincent Handon**, for all of the 1:00 a.m. telephone conversations, ideas, and encouragement. May your race on the rainbow track be filled with many treasures.

I am blessed to have you, **Bruce Ames, MD, Patricia Wilklund, Ph.D. and Harvey Alston,** in my life as my mentors. Thank you Bruce for the advice, support and friendship you have given me over the years. And thank you Patricia and Harvey for adopting me and coaching me to "Be the Best" in the speaking business.

Thank you, **Renee Simpson**, my good friend, for putting on the "white coat" when I just needed to vent. Over the years you have made a difference in my life. Always remember, you have the virtues that make champions. I love you always.

Thank you, **Don Starr**, my good friend and gifted graphic designer, for helping me complete this project. Wait until the world meets you!

To my editors, **Carol Starks, Adelia H. Williams, M.Ed., Ph.D.; Jennifer Collins; Seth Smiley; and Doreen Mannion**—thank you all.

# CONTENTS

Introduction vii

I. Breaking the Circles  1
   The Circle Breakers  7
   The Forgotten Circles  11
   The Virtues of Champions  13
   Overcoming Complacency  19
   The Dream Game  23

II. The Rainbow  29
    Symbols of the Rainbow  35
    Race Relations  37
    Desires for Peace  43

III. Motivation  49
     Staying Motivated  57
     Clubs, Organizations and Good People  63

IV. Desire: The Emotional Appetite For Success  73
    Facing A New Challenge  81
    Expressions of Desire  89
    Stress Reduction Through Sports  95
    A Tribute to Martin Luther King, Jr.  105
    Expression for Unity  115

V. Procrastination  121
   Asking the Right Questions  123
   Making the Decision  125
   A Closing Prayer  127

# INTRODUCTION

For many years now, a refreshing "can do" attitude has emerged within many individuals, a fresh perspective that can only be labeled a desire to achieve. If you find yourself reading this book, perhaps your new attitude has already emerged, and you are following your desire to succeed.

Success begins with wanting a fulfillment in our lives. We notice the prosperous ways to increase our occupational, spiritual, or financial freedom, but often we don't know how to achieve the increase that we desire. Surely, there are many people who find themselves in this situation. Nevertheless, we continue to hold on to our dreams.

We know that life is really about creating art, peace, love, and happiness—a personal fulfillment that can remain empty, until the proper action is taken to make things happen. We know something else as well; we know that to succeed we must risk failure—which doesn't mean fail, to succeed. It means know the consequences of the actions you take or moreover, the actions you don't take to succeed.

Having positive desires is the foundational key to all that we make happen in our lives. The following stories, affirmations, quotes, and antidotes are offered toward this fresh perspective. If it inspires you, if it encourages you to follow your dreams or creates unity, then pass on what it has done for you to others. All that any of us have to do is believe in ourselves, our vision, have a commitment, be patience, pursue, persist, and persevere.... and success can be yours.

— Melvin Murphy

Note: All stories are true. The names have been changed to protect the privacy of the individuals.

It isn't desire...

that keeps people trapped

it's the fear...

that they lack

the knowledge and ability

to succeed

-Melvin E. Murphy

*INDIVIDUAL ACTIONS...*
*ARE REQUIRED TO ACHIEVE SUCCESS.*

—Melvin Murphy

## BREAKING THE CIRCLES

What is a circle of desire? This phrase has been coined as having deep aspirations for greatness in a psychological image, but unable to break the invisible circle to achieve success while being economically, physically and socially trapped in disadvantaged conditions. Many people are faced with this situation because of impoverished backgrounds, education and social standing. Many people can visualize greatness mentally, but remain physically trapped because they do not take any action to break the circle.

There are times when a person can feel mentally trapped in an invisible glass circle of desire. A person can also mentally conceive of achieving all of their desired goals, but may not realize that they are indirectly trapped in an invisible glass circle. Nothing can stop a person from being successful, and this realization is what has to be brought into reality. Often, people can look at successful individuals around them and wonder when good things are going to happen to them. At times, people don't realize they are trapped in an invisible glass circle of desire looking out.

There are times when people may feel physically trapped in an invisible glass circle of desire like a mime actor who demonstrates being trapped behind an invisible wall. We as individuals also build invisible walls that can hinder our development process. Some people may feel they are shackled to a desk, performing the nine to five routine. This however, is only fine if that is their choice. Everyday, people want to physically begin their endeavors until once again they realize, indirectly, they are trapped in an invisible glass circle filled with desires that economically and socially are not within their reach—so they think.

Many people are mentally entangled in circles of desires. In discussions with friends and acquaintances, the subject of wanting to explore different economic avenues, new opportunities, or

## 2  Desire: The Emotional Appetite for Success

new possibilities, always seems far and in the distant future. Many people have the capabilities and resources to break the circles of desire, but are lacking in the areas of self-confidence, knowledge of the objectives, taking that first step in action, or missing the burning desire to be financially and emotionally free from their existence as the working poor in the land of opportunity—America.

There are individuals living slightly above or beneath the poverty line who can only see living for the moment and are afraid to take risks to reap the rewards. They no longer believe in the American dream; so they continue to allow their circumstances to govern their actions from breaking the circles through the winds of adversity and making their way into prosperity. At the writing of this chapter, there were 1.4 million (Statistical Abstract of the United States, 1993) adults living beneath the poverty line. An estimation of the adults living beneath the poverty line is 14 percent, many of whom are independent students. At times, they may find themselves living for the moment fueled by hope, knowing they will break their circles, in understanding this, the realization is, it's not lonesome in the circle.

Moreover, no one should allow the winds of adversity to dominate their actions from breaking the circles. They should constantly look at the bigger picture of having a slice of America's apple pie in any chosen endeavor. Constantly using self-motivating phases, such as "hang in there, believe in yourself," "you can do it," and "keep your eyes on the prize," it will happen, can be your bridge to reach the success you desire. We should constantly take some sort of action to make our dreams become reality, such as planning, brainstorming, or taking notes. This will allow us to refer to them when an idea is needed.

Individuals who wish to break the invisible circle of desire, to become successful at their endeavors, regardless of their economic makeup, position, or predicament, should contemplate this strategy in perspective:

1. **Have the desire.**

2. **Have a plan.**

3. Have a plan for action.

4. Have the desire to succeed.

5. Learn your craft.

Let's examine these strategies. What is desire? The Random House College Dictionary lists the meaning as to "express a wish to obtain; request or crave something." Plato, a great thinker said, "Desire is a single fund of energy which can be turned from one object to another like a stream diverted into another bed." There's a golden rule that manages the laws of desire. The rule elucidates that one can become, have, or achieve all that is desired if the desire is serious enough! In other words, one must be ardent for something, not a humble wish or mere wanting, but with a strong, eager, consuming desire that challenges defeat and demands fulfillment. Imagine you are an athlete who is always on the sidelines and your team is losing the game. That desire within you is saying, if only you had the chance to play, you could help your team to tie or win the game.

Desire motivates people to achieve success and be able to want for nothing or to experience the pleasures of what life has to offer independence, equality and the pursuit of happiness. You do not want to remain a player on the sideline of the game as one who does not get playing time. You must enthusiastically want to be victorious in your efforts. And creatively you must let it be known through your actions. Furthermore, the undiscovered creativity within oneself is a calling that can only be heed by the individual to take action. Talent such as sports, culinary skills, gardening, or what ever a person is skilled in, conceivably, is the key to breaking the circles. This undiscovered creativity, combined with life experiences, can be your super highway that grants passage to new and exciting possibilities.

Once a person realizes his or her hidden talents and capabilities, the sky is the limit on all that can be achieved. Once this realization has taken place, the thought must be embedded in the mind that one has the abilities to take action. Having the ability to look at one's own inner creativity isn't an art, but a requirement to be aware of what one enjoys doing.

What is a plan? Having a plan to attain your goals is merely having a plan of action, a road map which will guide you to your destination. Without the proper road map any road will take you anywhere, especially when you don't know where you're going. If the proper amount of time isn't allocated to planning sessions for your undertakings, you will feel as if you are on a roller coaster. One minute you're up presuming that everything is coming along great, until something you didn't plan for surprisingly develops. The next minute you're headed down, ending in a major catastrophic failure which could force your project to be terminated.

In your plans, there should be a market analysis, marketing strategies, potential problem areas, and financial plans. All first time business starters must be concerned with these areas. Having a well thought out plan is a critical component of any venture to help reduce the potential pitfalls.

What is a plan of action? The action plan is simply setting in motion the plans for your endeavor by starting an action to make things happen to achieve the outcome that you desire. By beginning the activity, you will enhance the visualization of your dream and make it appear all the more real and attainable. Always keep in mind that the road to success is paved with objections. No matter how prepared you are in the planning or implementing the start up, the results will be slow. Meanwhile, continue step-by-step until you reach your goal. Procrastination is the adversary of success (Procrastination discussed in Ch. 5).

During this period, you must reinforce your decision to overcome obstacles. With every bit of energy you can muster, coupled with steadfastness, envision your endeavors succeeding. Do not allow your goals to linger in the planning stage. More often than not, successful entrepreneurs and business executives must be committed and determined to provide a good service or product, and, most importantly, take the necessary action to begin their ventures.

Learning the craft, vocation, or skill is critical to your success. If you do not know enough about the field you have selected, enroll in courses, read several books, articles, and trade magazines to help you become an authority in your field. Joining clubs, organizations and associations will enhance your networking and give you a chance to talk with people who are doing what you want to do. Also, joining organizations will keep you up-to-date with industry practices, changes, and events.

Learning your craft proficiently along with producing a quality product or service will enhance your longevity in any profession. For example, every year in the music industry uncommitted singing groups and solo acts make their one record, receive their fifteen minutes of fame, and disappear, never to be heard from again. This can be for many reasons, focusing on the aspect of quality, some musical artists will get in the recording studio and allow the technology to sing for them until it's time to sing live and on stage. Then the quality of sound and performance of the artist is unsatisfactory. Bad practices such as this will cause any musical career to be over before it gets started. To solve this problem, young and new artists in all occupations, projects and ventures should allow themselves time to learn and develop their skills.

Why are you doing the work you are currently doing? Breaking the circles of desire on your present job can be the first step to achieving success, if you decide to remain with your company. If a decision has been made to continue employment with your present employer, you should make the commitment to excel to a higher position. If a decision to try other avenues has been made, excelling in your present job can only be a benefit, such as having additional money to finance your project(s) through salary increases, gaining recognition as an accomplished worker, and making higher echelon contacts.

One method of prevailing on your current job is to find approaches to make your job more efficient, productive, and cost effective for the company. Creativity can only come from the individual. Creating a way of saving money for any company will cause upper management to take notice of your abilities and your dedication to the company's mission and objectives.

Another method is to determine why you like or dislike your

job. Once you find the answers, begin working diligently to improve upon your weakest areas. Often, we allow our dislikes to fall below standards and this shows on our performance evaluations. Remember, always work harder on the areas you do not like. Why? Simply, because you don't like them.

Finally, having the desire to succeed means you feel the need to achieve, to win, or to fulfill your dreams. Accomplishing your goals and witnessing your creation come to life will give you absolute gratification and a feeling of accomplishment. By taking the action, enduring the opposition, and gaining the rewards of a successful venture, you have captured the essence of experiencing what life has to offer—prosperity. At this point, you may feel ready to begin your next endeavor or maybe not, regardless, you now have the self-confidence, tenacity, and a positive mental attitude to take on any future challenges.

When taking on new challenges, timing is of major importance. Timing is important because others in your chosen field are out there being resourceful to start their venture too. For instance, if your venture is seasonal, accurate planning to start is crucial to your success. Timing can be important especially if your venture is too far behind the industry standards or too far advanced.

Finding a window of opportunity is important. That window of opportunity can be how you decide to start your venture. For example, we'll use the occupation of public speaking. Public speaking opportunities are usually gained through referral or name recognition. Referrals will come after others have heard you speak.

Name recognition will come by what you do to gain publicity for yourself. Meanwhile, if you don't have a name that is publicly recognizable, plan to start your venture around the holidays or events that gain media coverage—this will give you free advertisement and start your name recognition. Also, the timing has to be well planned or you'll miss your unique window of opportunity.

*BEWARE OF EASY SOLUTIONS.*

—*Vincent Sheehy*

## THE CIRCLE BREAKERS

Breaking the invisible circle of desire usually comes through extreme trials and tribulations. Many people have and will migrate from extreme financial broken backgrounds. However, having a positive state of mind—a person can achieve anything.

There are several people who have allowed their positive mental attitudes to break the circle of desire and have made United States history. Carol Moseley-Braun, Joycelyn Elders and Nelson Mandela, broke their circle of desires and changed the political arena forever. Carol Moseley-Braun broke her circle of desire by becoming the first African American woman nominated by the Democratic party to win a Senate primary race. Senator Moseley-Braun took action and has become a symbol to all women, men and minorities, signifying that America remains a land of opportunity for all of its citizens.

Before the Senate race, Moseley-Braun's desires went beyond her job as Recorder of Deeds in Cook County, Ill. She was animate about moving into an arena where she could make a difference. Senator Moseley-Braun has accomplished what many people desire to achieve; the only difference is Senator Carol Moseley-Braun took the action to make things happen and so should you.

In another case, Joycelyn Elders, being black, female and born to poor sharecroppers in a rural section of Schaal, Arkansas, was not discouraged from becoming a success. Elders broke her circle of desire by overcoming barriers which eventually led to her being highly respected in the field of pediatric endocrinology. Acquiring an education was difficult and challenging for Joycelyn Elders. After completing chores of cotton picking, she had a daily journey of five miles to ride the school bus that took her thirteen miles to an all black high school.

Elders graduated from high school and went on to attend Philander Smith College, also an all black institution. Joycelyn paid her tuition by cleaning floors. While cleaning floors, Elders discovered her love for biology and chemistry but surrendered emotionally to the fact that all she would be was a laboratory aide; until she attended a lecture by the first black woman to attend the University of Arkansas School of Medicine—Edith Irby Jones. At that point in time, Elders knew that her desire to be a doctor would be a reality. Why? Because she witnessed that it had been done and believed she could do it—but better.

After graduating from college, Dr. Elders enlisted in the U. S. Army with the purpose of obtaining the G. I. Bill which was to pay for medical School. After serving several years, and with her G. I. Bill in hand, Joycelyn Elders attended the University of Arkansas School of Medicine as one of three blacks and the only female. In 1993, Joycelyn Elders was nominated for the position of U. S. Surgeon General by President Bill Clinton. Dr. Elders held the highest-ranking public health post an African American and a woman has ever held. "We are trying to develop a health care system that will provide primary care for all" said Elders.

∽

In 1962, a young man name Nelson Mandela was incarcerated for five years. In Cape Town, South Africa, Nelson Mandela spent years in prison for the incitement to strike and to leave the country without a valid passport. In 1964, Mandela was sentenced to life in prison for sabotage and conspiracy to overthrow the South African government. At the prime of his youth, Mandela served twenty-seven years in jail.

In 1990, Nelson Mandela with failing health was unconditionally released, from prison. As soon as Mandela was released, the African National Congress [ANC] and other liberation organizations were formed under Nelson Mandela's leadership. Two years later and a multitude of negotiations, Mandela and South Africa's President Frederick W. de Klerk, adopted a new constitution that would outlaw apartheid and make all citizens equal under law. In 1994, Nelson Mandela, at the age of seventy-five, was elected as South Africa's first black president.

Through Mandela's long and drawn out pilgrimage from being a political prisoner and a prisoner of state, he is now the head of state that jailed him most of his life. His goals became his driving force to succeed. The lesson in these stories—if you have the desire, belief, determination and perseverance in yourself and in your cause, no matter what trials or tribulations are placed upon you, keep in your heart the faith that if there is a will, there is a way.

∽

Talk show host, Sally Jessy Raphael is a decorated veteran at professional failures—within her first ten years as a broadcaster she held twenty-four jobs and was terminated from eighteen of them. Some people can't imagine being fired from one job, let alone being fired from eighteen. After discovering her niche, her desire, fortitude, conviction and impetus awarded her an Emmy in 1989; and pushed her into the race, as one of the hottest syndicated talk show hosts in the television industry.

Raphael is an excellent example of what perseverance and determination can do—if one door is closed, open another and another, and keep on keeping on until you find what you're searching to gain.

∽

Professional tennis player, Pete Sampras, without a high school diploma, at the age of nineteen, became the youngest sportsman to win the largest grand prize in America—the U. S. Open. Two weeks after that victorious win, Sampras was dethroned in the quarterfinal by friend Jim Courier. Labeled as lacking"the stuff legends are made of" two years later—in 1993, Sampras walked away with "two Grand Slam titles and became the world's number one ranked player," clinching the number one position from his friend Courier. While on a roll, Pete decided to win "his third Grand Slam at Center Court at Flushing Meadow—disposing of rival Cedric Pioline. As an amateur, Pete was labeled as "a good but not outstanding junior player." His desire proved them wrong.

∽

Rigoberta Menchu, an Indian woman, born poor and raised in the fincas-a plantation with barely no food "has had more than enough motivation to activism: the torture and assassination of her father, mother, and younger brother bear witness to the kind of strong-arm rule of the Guatemalan government forces—a rule that has literally held captive the indians of that country, and one that Menchu has fought for more than ten years." Rigoberta virtually had no childhood and did not attend school. But through the enormous paths of abuse, hunger, fear, and a devastated homeland, Menchu's motivation has forced her to become a human-rights activist. A job well done—has awarded her the title of Nobel laureate. Through a translator, she has written her autobiography, *I, Rigoberta Menchu*. The autobiography tells of her plight coming from a hard world and the others she tried to save.

The lesson in these stories are, no matter how many doors you must open, nor how many tennis balls you must hit, nor the level of education you have, or what labels people place upon you, nor the feeling of hopelessness or helplessness—of power—that an individual has "is more a matter of attitude than of objective fact." An individual can achieve more,"for themselves and for others, when they believe they can; and every failure should be viewed" as building blocks to give you a firm foundation for something greater to come. Do not "lapse into despair when you believe that nothing you can do will really make any difference" and every failure becomes a discovery and a test of your desires and commitment—remember that all your efforts will make the difference in succeeding.

*IF YOU ONLY LOOK AT WHAT IS, YOU MIGHT NEVER ATTAIN WHAT COULD BE.*

—*Unknown*

## THE FORGOTTEN CIRCLES

Breaking the circles of desire into prosperity will not mean wealth, affluence or an enormous amount of monetary or material accumulation to some people. There are many people breaking the circles of desire that have achieved great success because they made a decision to try. Many go unheard of because they are not blockbuster movie stars, famous singers, politicians or high paid athletes. Others go unheard of because they are struggling to obtain the basic needs for survival on a daily basis. For illustration, a woman who has children and lived under a street bridge and in shelters carrying her entire life in plastic bags, and ragged old suitcases—manages to pull herself from cardboard boxes and the dangers that accompanies that penury lifestyle—gets a low paying job, government subsidize housing and public schooling for her family is a success; or the people with AIDS who are fighting for their lives and surviving year after year, beating the odds or whatever you want. And the precious children who are stricken with terminal illnesses survive another six months—they are a success.

We must remember the law enforcement officers who risk their lives daily in the criminal environment—arrive home safely to their families one more time; or the firemen and women who bravely walk into burning houses and buildings to rescue people are a success; or the rescue teams who see death and destruction everyday and manage to keep their sanity, and neighborhood watch groups who risk retaliation from drug pushers, prostitutes and the neighborhood violence—because they have made the commitment to take back the communities and streets—they are a success.

Success in breaking the circle of desire appears in many shapes, forms and sizes. The breaking of circles of desires, emerge in the shape of being able to live life one more day. The circle of desire surfaces in the form of providing for the ones you love. The circle of desire comes when you protect or save a life or begin to make peace and harmony in our neighborhoods; this can lead everyone to enjoy living through each breath of life, only if an attempt is made.

*THE SUN AND MOON INTERACT WITH ONE ANOTHER VERY PRECISELY TO SHOW DIFFERENT ACHIEVEMENTS ESSENTIAL IN LIFE.*

—*Melvin Murphy*

## THE VIRTUES OF CHAMPIONS

In everyone's life a feeling occurs to want—a feeling to be successful. A feeling of being unsure of your future. A feeling when all ambition, all expectations, all motivation, all perseverance, and all involvement are forced to be relinquished. Many have allowed these disappointments to shatter their dreams; others have employed these qualities as building blocks to support their successful endeavors.

The distinction between people who surrender to the disappointments of failure and the people who achieve success over failure are the people who do not discontinue their efforts. In the beginning or midst of an undertaking, people surrender their wants to the negative forces and the unpopular opinions of others. Many of our closest friends and relatives find it exceedingly difficult to picture us as entrepreneurs, top business executives, or even motivational writers—I'm now speaking of individuals who constantly dance with unwanted disappointments and are labeled as being confused or don't know what to do with their lives.

Others surrender while in the middle of their undertakings because the pressure feels like driving a car with the emergency brakes on. After a while, the pressure is insufferable and termination of the activities is inevitable. Many individuals do not aspire to make their dreams or goals become reality for various reasons. Conversely, many people who acquire success remain focused, dedicated, and determined to see their dreams come to life—or perhaps in a small way, to prove to the disbelievers that they can be successful in their new venture. Today, men and women attain their goals through planning, education, and hard work.

In addition, the power of positive thinking is utilized more than ever to help individuals achieve success. Moreover, it is the desire to have which starts the emotions to want. Every individual who desires to break the invisible glass circle, regardless of the vocation, must possess certain cardinal virtues such as: Discipline, Courage, Wisdom, Open-mindedness, Justice, Fortitude, Courtesy and Friendship. Having these virtues isn't a guarantee to secure success, but it's an excellent starting place. Let's examine these virtues in detail:

*Discipline.* The key to success is self-discipline. Discipline is simply self-control. "For a person to possess self control, the better portion of his [or her] character must control the weaker part in order to rein in his [or her] desires." In other words, we often focus on our abilities while ignoring our weaker areas. Such as, not attempting to learn all the material(s) which pertain to our undertaking—basically we must become experts in the rules and regulations of our chosen fields, especially if we don't know all of the rules. For example, a medical doctor cannot learn about half of the human body and be considered a medical doctor. They must learn the entire anatomy of the human body, even if they specialize in one area of the human body. Medical doctors must endure hundreds of hours of comprehensive training throughout their careers and many will attest to every hard working hour. To sum it up, you must have the discipline to improve upon your weaker areas that are needed to be successful.

*Courage.* The courage of a person is manifested in bravery or fearlessness. Courage is a state of mind, when individuals are challenged with unknown circumstances this state enables a great deal of confidence to guide them through enormous difficulties and risk. Difficulties such as the inspiring entrepreneur leaving the job security of a major corporation to pursue dreams of being self-employed, without a regular pay check or benefits, is a large difficulty to overcome. Within many of us exists courage and the belief that we will not fail and set out to conquer the entrepreneurial world. Happily, 10 percent will succeed. Sadly, 90 percent will fail for assorted reasons; however, the total percentage of those who attempt any venture and has failed at least had the courage to try.

The risk always lies in the failure of the endeavor and falling from grace in the eyes of your peers. Having courage and the emotional feeling of knowing that you can succeed, if you take the risk, is just like eating from a box of assorted chocolate covered candies—you don't always know what you're getting, but you do know it will be sweet. Many individuals have chosen to take the risk and they are happy that they are now in control of their own destinies. In other words, try a piece of candy.

*Wisdom.* "In the perfect man [or woman] reason will rule, with the spirited element as its auxiliary over the bodily appetites." Having the understanding of good judgment and knowledge is a basic foundation in being successful. To get the knowledge desired, many people attend universities and colleges with the notion that a degree will give them all information and the unalienable right to have a job and be successful—which is far from being true. Many college and university graduates must understand that a degree is only considered to be a fishing license—it will allow you to fish, it doesn't mean you will catch any fish.

*ATTITUDE IS ALTITUDE....HOW FAR YOU GET IN LIFE.*

—*Unknown*

Given that humans are not perfect, a man or woman must profit from knowledge by way of life experiences, nourishing the knowledge already gained, and continuing their education after college by attending seminars, company in-house training and the like. Because the amount you can earn is determined by how much you can learn, in your career. Keep in mind the amount earned doesn't necessarily have to be in the monetary perception; it can be in the spiritual, emotional or mental perception. Proverbs 1:2, *"to know wisdom and instruction; to perceive the words of understanding"*—in other words, wisdom put to good use is power and can be more valuable than gold.

*Open-mindedness.* Having an open mind is like opening a window to receive fresh air on a windy day. Opening the eyes of the mind allows a flow of cognizance or logic which empowers each of us to communicate with one another. Opening the mind's eye enables all people to see, feel, and gain experiences in peace, love, beauty and knowledge which is apart of life.

Having an open mind to receive fresh, and new information will enable people to broaden their horizons by sharing—current events, success stories, and making long-lasting true friends through communications. Keep in mind that open-mindedness borders on increasing wisdom. Always be willing to learn and share new ideas, regardless of anyone's opinions, because what you learn from others may help in your future activities.

*Justice.* Justice emerges not only as a matter of external behavior towards others, but as an internal order of the spirit from which proper behavior will eventually follow. In other words, if a person has honesty, truth and beauty in their heart, it will shine like the sun on a nice summer day. To carry yourself with integrity leads others to trust and have faith in you. In truth there is verity; always demonstrate verity—this will differentiate you from others. Beauty is a human need and a special trait; we often see beauty in things that please us and often cannot find beauty in those things that do not please us. Each of us should always search for beauty within ourselves because when you are beautiful, you will be loved, and when you are loved, you will love. Open your eyes and heart to beauty—humanly and with nature and create harmony among all people. Justice comes from within, and should be displayed on the level with everyone in your life—your family, friends, adversaries, business associates and most importantly to yourself—you must always stand for something or you'll fall for anything.

*Fortitude.* Fortitude is self-regarding. Fortitude commands us to tolerate and endure hardships for hopes of achieving a good life for ourselves and our families. Constantly fortifying one's own belief is important; and without this moral virtue we cannot effectively pursue our dreams.

For example, when baking a cake the key ingredient is flour. Mixing the secondary ingredients, eggs, sugar, and butter are important—but nothing will hold all of the ingredients together to make a cake except flour. So, in relation, flour represents the fortitude that will hold you together in difficult times in your life and in your endeavors.

In another sense, how does one maintain fortitude? This

question is answered by simply saying, it depends on what you are trying to accomplish and the goals you have established for yourself. If there is one area to concentrate on to help give you impetus or strength—it would be physical health. It is important to be healthy if you plan to take on projects that require high energy for success.

Why? In any enterprise that requires major responsibility, like making scheduled meetings on time, meeting deadlines under pressure, or being the primary on a campaign, needs a dependable person—having faulty health could slow down your activity and cause possible failure. Again, fortitude is the vitamin that will give you strength, to help hold it all together.

*Courtesy.* Courtesy is a virtue that will escalate you to new heights, only if it is utilized on a constant and sincere basis and with the people you are in contact with. Having a polite behavior or being well mannered towards others, will automatically compel people to want to be associated with you. There isn't a middle of the road when it comes to courtesy; either you are courteous or you're not. Make it a good habit to practice courtesy.

*Friendship.* Friendship is important to most people. People who do not have friends for whatever reasons will be lonely people. Having and making friends provides a feeling of brotherhood and sisterhood. Having trustworthy friends can be closer to you than a sister or brother.

Selecting friends can be a demanding responsibility—however a responsibility that is a necessity. Choosing good friends will relieve you of worries who you can trust. When selecting your friends, select them by their actions towards you and others. Having a good group of friends can lead to a great many rewards—the most important being trust, love and respect. Remember, in order to have good friends, one must first be a good friend.

Having these virtues of champions increases your determination to win at your project(s) and at any milestone(s) in your life. Having discipline keeps you working toward your aspirations. Having courage allows you to withstand the doubts of others, and the adversities that may lie ahead. Having wisdom will be a firm foundation to building your empire.

Having justice allows others to trust you and being open-minded permits you to accept fresh ideas and enhance your communications. Having fortitude is a key ingredient in helping you hold it all together while having genuine courtesy towards others affords you the opportunity to associate with good people. Being a good friend allows you to make good friends.

*On your mark, ready, set...begin.*

—Melvin Murphy

## Overcoming Complacency

What is complacency? Complacency is the feeling of being content. Often we resign ourselves to the circumstances we have been dealt—such as remaining in unproductive situations that hinder our personal growth and development. Some individuals become complacent in their current situation and are fearful of making any major changes in their lives. Because change can be frightening, we don't always know what the consequences will be. Many people choose to remain in a situation because that complacency becomes a crutch of security.

For example, many people go to their places of employment every day knowing they are not happy. This may create great levels of stress and tension. Many people may feel there isn't any growth or creativity in their jobs anymore. Some may remain in the same position because of their economic situation, which is understandable if they don't know what they really want to do next in their careers or if they are afraid of change.

To overcome complacency, you must take action or have a purpose that will lead to action. If you have a positive idea, or a rising desire, you should act on it; this can be your opportunity to make the changes that you have been longing for. Don't wait for your ship to come in, because you must first send one out to make room for another one to come in.

When is it time to stop being complacent? In reference to an occupation, the time is when you are unhappy. The time is right when your mental and physical health are at risk. People should remember that corporations are downsizing and this is forcing the workers that remain employed to work extra hours—essentially carrying the workload of two people. The time is right when a person is ready—only an individual can identify when enough is enough. The time is right when an unproductive situation is no longer mutually beneficial to both parties involved.

Change can be good. It allows us to not become complacent

in our daily lives. Although some people will resist change like rushing to the dentist—to sit under a drill. Others welcome positive changes and perceive change as growth. Today, we are living in a society where change can be a requirement; for instance, every one to three years corporations must keep up with technology—so they must purchase updated software packages to remain competitive or apply changes to the mainframe computer called upgrades. Corporations do this because it becomes a necessity—so change could be a necessity for you too.

Life is full of changes. We change days of the week, months of the year and we even change the number of the year. The days of the week will continue to change, the months of the year will continue to change, even the year will continue to change—but if you are reluctant to make beneficial changes in your life and remain in unconstructive situations that impede your dreams, goals or aspirations, the days will come, the months will come, and the years will come and go without you. You will remain at a standstill. So don't fan the fire of misery, make a positive change in your life.

How do you recognize positive change? Positive change is recognized by identifying the situation or the results affected by the change. Positive change is recognized in some situations more easily than others—as when a cigarette smoker quits smoking. Although the ex-smoker may see or experience a definite mood swing, quitting is a recognizable positive change.

It is good when we are able to observe positive changes immediately, it's the best form of instant gratification; however, some changes can take years or even a lifetime to complete—as when an adult who did not receive a secondary education finds it difficult to progress or be competitive in the global work world and recognizes the vast need to educate himself. Too often in a "hurry up and wait" mode or have an "I want it now" attitude. We must force ourselves to remember that it takes time to get an education, build a business or a career—or write a motivational book—and we should reacquaint ourselves with patience. If we keep diligently performing the duties it takes to accomplish our goals and have plenty of patience, change will come—just as the dew appears on the morning glory after a night of rain.

Be patient, keep working and change will come.

There are times when people remain complacent in their careers, dreams, and in their personal lives, because they have low self-esteem. Having assurance in yourself and in your capabilities is what fuels the desire to be successful. And if you have a shortage of this fuel, you most certainly can't heat up your desire to succeed. Case in point: a young, gifted, self-taught artist set out to gain exposure for his works. He acquired a wall in a busy local coffee shop and spent the following two months painting and preparing for this great opportunity and free advertisement.

His artistry remained affixed to the wall for a month and received positive reviews from the customers who frequented the establishment. The owner of the shop allowed the paintings to remain on the wall for an additional month and asked the artist to paint three additional portraits, at a price of nine hundred dollars each. The artist's hard work had paid off... so you would think. Unfortunately, the artist's self-esteem was so low that he did not want to charge the owner for the paintings he had been asked to paint.

The point here is that all of the artist's creative time, effort and exposure went down the drain, just as if he had unplugged a sink full of water after washing dishes. His low self-esteem stopped him from completing his goals and he remains complacent at the place where he started.

To overcome a self-esteem problem, you must first, recognize that you are capable of reaching your objectives. Always believe in yourself and in your talents. If you still have a hard time with your emotions, then consider seeking counseling.

*Seize a moment to dream...and when you dream...dream big or don't dream at all.*

—*Melvin Murphy*

## THE DREAM GAME

What is a dream? A dream is a fantasy, illusion, aspiration or vision of hope for something. A dream can be something beautiful, enchanting, refreshing, or it can be an internal message to follow your desires. A dream can be considered attainable or realistically achievable.

When you find yourself dreaming, it's often because you have a deep desire to acquire something wonderful. For example, in most large metropolitan cities where the lottery game is played, people wish for the numbers they have selected to be drawn, so they can follow their dreams. It is normal to hear someone say, "I wish I could win the lottery." It's a way of securing your beliefs to obtain your desires.

To further enhance your beliefs about securing your dreams, play the dream game—an action game. For the next twenty days follow the dream game plan. You must play this game with the desire and zeal to win. If you feel you lack the characteristics needed to play, then re-read the section on Virtues of Champions to help with your self-confidence.

If you miss a day or week, continue where you dropped the ball and complete the remaining weeks. On your mark, ready, set...begin.

**WEEK ONE**

1. **Identify your dream.**

What is your goal? What do you desire most? What is your objective? Find a quiet place where you will not be disturbed or interrupted. Take a note pad to jot down your ideas. Jot down all of your desires or goals. Try to be as accurate as possible in describing what you want. You can write down as many goals as you want.

Once you have listed your desires, number them in order of importance from one to ten and so forth. Disregard goals below the number of three—place them on the back burner for later. Take the remaining three choices and reclassify them in order of importance again. Think very carefully and seriously. Disregard numbers two and three—and focus your time and attention on the number one priority. Remember, do not discuss your ideas with anyone—you do not need any opposing opinions at this stage, unless it's someone (a mentor) in the field you have chosen or someone you can depend on to motivate you to continue. Keep your notebook in a secure place.

**WEEK TWO**

2. **Analyze your dream's environment.**

To be successful with your dream you must know what is happening in the environment. Determine what the competition is up to, and decide if there is a need for your dream in the area you have chosen.

3. **Identify the opportunities and threats.**

After you have analyzed your dream's environment, evaluate what you have learned in the form of opportunities.

**WEEK THREE**

4. **Analyze your dream's resources.**

What skills, abilities, and education do you need to be successful? What is your cash position? How can you raise capital—money to finance your dream?

5. **Identify your dream's strengths and weaknesses.**

What courses and training can you take to gain knowledge on your objective? Determine your competitive products or services.

**WEEK FOUR**

6. **Reassess your dreams or objectives.**

Are they realistic? Do they need any adjustments? Where does adjustment need to be made? Ask yourself, "Am I ready to formulate a game plan?" "What is my commitment level?"

7. **Formulate a game plan.**

How will you put your dream into action?

8. **Implement your game plan.**

Start the game plan and play to win.

Once you have completed the dream game, you are well on your way to acquiring the success you deserve. Remember, always dream. It doesn't cost anything to dream, it's one of the few things that remains free—remember, the only problem with dreaming is that you give yourself everything. Realistically, stick to the one dream you desire most. Good luck and congratulations on making the team as a DREAMER.

The world is full of beauty

but

nothing is more beautiful

than a

multitude of colors.

-Melvin E. Murphy

*THE BEAUTY OF THE GROUP LIES IN ITS SIMPLE UNITY.*

—W. E. B. DuBois

## THE RAINBOW

The mystical colors appearing in the sky against the sun after a rainfall or within a mist is a rainbow. The arc-shaped mist has the colors of red, orange, yellow, green, blue, indigo and violet aligned accurately, side-by-side, in harmony. In this section, the colors of the rainbow will represent, in abstract, those people who are constantly working, living, and struggling together to achieve a declaration of universal love among all nations. Also, it represents the starting point on an Olympic meter track, with the finishing line crossing into the land of hope, peace, and unity for all people running the race.

The rainbow covers the world. It comes without hatred, racism, hate crimes, prejudices, political correctness, or judgments, and without a price to those who wish to enjoy its beauty. The rainbow is a constant reminder of the wonders that we can achieve as a force, in unison, by striving toward a common and universal goal of harmony. There are several times a year when people forcefully seek to unite—especially Christmas and Thanksgiving. During the week before Thanksgiving, some people make every effort to feed the hungry—not taking into consideration that they are also hungry the other three hundred sixty days of the year. I don't include in this category those individuals and organizations who are overworked, understaffed, and whose mission is to provide provisions on a daily basis—we applaud you and encourage you to keep up the good efforts.

We even set a special day aside to share love—that day is Valentine's Day. On Valentine's Day, we shower our loved ones with flowers, candy and cards—which is good, but don't allow material gratuities to speak for you. Why not? Because the beautiful flowers will inevitably die; the candy will be eaten or allowed to sit and become stale—if it's not frozen; the cards will either be stored in a box out of sight or discarded into the garbage. All of it will ultimately disappear. If you do not have love deep within your heart or compassion in your soul, the flowers, candy and cards will not sustain your relationship throughout the year. Also, we should take time for those less fortunate people who don't have a loved one in their lives. Shower the less fortunate with the most expensive gift you can give—your free TIME. Giving your time to someone who is in need of a friend, companion, or mentor is a priceless gift. It demonstrates how highly they are valued. We often maintain we're too busy in our everyday lives to donate time to people who are on the edge of falling between the crevices of society into crime, depression, or are just lonely. Yet we can spend a great deal of money and countless hours of planning to make sure we get our cars and trucks serviced. Give the same amount of time and planning to save a child or help someone who is in need of guidance or teach someone to believe in themselves—"*Ye ought to support the weak.*" Acts 20:35

There isn't a man-made law that requires a person to be wealthy in order to be a philanthropist. Philanthropy comes in many different forms and contributions other than giving money. You are a philanthropist if you volunteer, give, donate or contribute your time freely, to help, aid and assist others without charging a price for your services. You are also a philanthropist if you donate your company's services.

Let's not forget spending time with our elders who are in retreat villages and nursing homes. They have our history, and it's a joyful occasion to sit and talk with them about the past—they are our inspiration and we can still learn from them, so that we will not make the same mistakes and allow bad history to repeat itself. Take the time to make a visit, because one day it may be you who needs a visitor. One of the greatest gifts you can receive from anyone is the gift of a smile when you have made someone happy.

Allow the feelings of joy, happiness and the giving of oneself as it is felt on holidays—feelings that should be disseminated every day—allow them to become the everyday norm—just as the military raises the American flag every morning at sunrise to show honor for our country and our men in uniform. Allow the giving of self to be apparent—such as greeting your fellow man and woman. Acknowledge their presence or existence when you approach or pass them for the first time by simply saying "good morning" or the appropriate salutation for the time of day. For example, many times there are two people in an elevator and they will not acknowledge one another—mostly because of the fear of crime; however, we cannot allow crime to govern how we treat one another or commit to greeting each other—a personal greeting shows respect.

The point being, if the rainbow can display its beauty unconditionally around the world, then why can't we display our love unconditionally and more often? We must try to make every day Thanksgiving Day, Valentine's Day or even Christmas Day. One designated day to show love is clearly not enough to spread love. Our world is always open to revisions; let's revise the meanings of these holidays by making every day a holiday—make holidays more than just a day off from work.

A myth about the rainbow is that there is a pot of gold at the end of it—what comes to mind are shiny gold coins, the size of fifty-cent pieces, filling the pot to the brim; and, "How can I find that valuable pot?" If you found that pot of gold, you would certainly spend some of it, risk some on the stock market, invest some of it, and you would deposit some in a bank to draw interest.

However, who to say that the pot at the end of the rainbow is filled with shiny gold coins? The pot that sits at the end of the beautiful arc can be filled with various treasures more valuable than gold, such as finding the opportunity to fulfill your dreams, an opportunity camouflaged as hard work; overcoming obstacles by having hope discovering or re-discovering friendships and love of family; or finding a coat of honesty and honor.

The contents in the rainbow pot are whatever each individual seeks to discover. If peace, love and happiness are what you crave, then you must decide what it will take to make that happen for you. If you desire to be successful in your ventures, find out what it takes to prevail. Or maybe you lack appreciation for what you already have—don't spend time thinking about what you don't have; instead, spend time appreciating what you do have.

It is natural to spend a great deal of time thinking about the things you desire out of life. But don't spend too much time pondering, because this can cause you to be more concerned with thinking about having something than with the thought of planning how to achieve getting something. Also, this can cause you to ignore the things you have already accumulated. Take the time to appreciate the things you have, because you can always become worse off by losing what you have already achieved.

Now that you probably realize you can find a portion of your rainbow treasures within yourself and in what you already have, by all means spend some of it, risk some on your private stock market, invest some of it, and certainly deposit some in a bank to gain interest for when you need it on that rainy day.

What is the pot at the end of the rainbow? The pot at the end of the rainbow is what you want personally for your life. No matter how hard someone else tries to make you happy—if you don't seek your own treasure, you won't find happiness. Individually, we must take the journey to find our own rainbow pot.

How can we find the rainbow's pot of treasures? We can find valuable treasures by taking a journey—a life journey. No one person can give the true treasures you desire, so each of us must pursue our own dreams on the Olympic track through the life cycle—whether we are successful or whether we meet with failure, each of us must get on that track. As you proceed along the rainbow track you will become experienced in the game of life. By the time you walk, run, or take a stroll to the end of the rainbow track, you will have earned your treasures along the way.

Your journey will allow you to experience the trials, tribulations, obstacles, and pitfalls. It will teach you to transform difficulties into glorious discoveries of what life has to offer. For instance, every day of our lives we learn or experience something new by way of the television, newspapers, radio, through hard work, college, magazines, friends or acquaintances—the list is endless. We store all that we have gained and experienced in our minds for later use.

However, all gained experiences allow us to decide what goals we desire, and compel us to obtain them. Moreover, that's why the pot is at the end of the rainbow—you may place the bits and pieces of your life journey and its treasures in the pot. Once you have filled your pot with the riches of success, you will become a symbol of achievement to others and the earning of your treasures symbolizes finding the pot of gold at the end of the rainbow.

In essence, you can't aspire to find a physical pot of gold until you create one as you travel through the life cycle with each step through life. Always look within your heart with a positive mind and conduct a self inventory. You may be surprised to find you now have more than you had before and that you're not the same person you used to be—you're better than before.

Today, we live in a constant state of shock. All we see on the television news is meaningless violence. All we hear about are white collar crimes committed by elected officials in public office—which overshadows the honest, hardworking officials who are still dedicated to serving the public interest. Every day the news is saturated with crime statistics of local killings, drug raids, and robberies. Crime on the news has become social conversation and it's sad that America is more interested in what goes on in other people's bedrooms, or hearing about the shattered dreams of a falling celebrity, than the state of affairs of our communities and country. We allow the good news in our communities to be placed on page twenty of the newspapers and the bad news to placed on the front page. We are allowing the bad news to overshadow the good news, all just to make money. For example, we constantly hear of teenagers committing crimes, but we rarely hear of the teenagers doing the right things, staying out of trouble and away from substance abuse. We must pay homage to the well-behaved teenagers more often, because it's harder for them to remain crime and drug-free, especially with the amount of peer pressure they face daily. We must continually fortify their decision to keep doing the right things to succeed and become productive citizens by acknowledging their good deeds.

On the other hand, we must rescue the others who have fallen into the crevices of society. We must work with them outside of the school system by instilling excitement of life, success through education, communication, and with self-motivation. (Motivation will be covered in Ch. 3.) The rainbow can be a symbol of creation, of what is to come—such as your dreams or goals. The rainbow has a different interpretation to different people or the connotation of the rainbow to many people conveys a similar meaning, in association with life—to ascertain love, peace, happiness, wealth, and equality for all mankind.

The rainbow has its scientific rational for how and why it exists. If you need a clear understanding of what the rainbow can mean, consider the rainbow as a tapestry. It has many different colored threads intertwined to create a representation. In other words, the colors and threads are working collectively to consummate a purpose—they have become one entity to accomplish one overall goal—to become a beautiful picture.

We can also work collectively to complete a goal. We must not be concerned about pleasing the critics, but be greatly concerned with doing whatever is needed to get the job done—to bring unity among all people during these troubled times. We must emotionally support one another during the difficult times.

To create a rainbow, it takes both the rain and sunshine. In abstract this means there will be ups and downs when we begin to make changes; nevertheless, even in times of hopelessness, we must continue to have a vision. We have been dispirited long enough in this world; now is the time to become high-spirited and make changes for the better.

*Tolerance is not enough...but acceptance is.*

— *Melvin Murphy*

## Symbols of the Rainbow

Image is everything when sending a message, whether it's struggling to gain civil rights or selling a consumer product. People are very protective of their image for many reasons. Some will hold themselves to a higher standard because of their occupation, such as being a television reporter, a politician, a high profile business executive, a member of a well known organization. People protect their image because they are often judged by their actions and character—this often carries a more superficial connotation.

A group of people have employed the colors of the rainbow to represent their image. They have entrusted the rainbow colors to signify unity among all people. They have even chosen diversity to be a solid infrastructure for achieving acceptance, equal rights, love and peace worldwide. They are the men and women in the gay and lesbian communities. Most people living the alternative lifestyle are constantly subjected to negative stereotypes about their communities and lifestyle. They are ridiculed, trivialized, discriminated against, physically abused, mentally raped, and made to feel inconsequential for loving one another. These stereotypes emerge mainly from the media—television and newspapers. Often, the gay newspapers and magazines stereotype their own lifestyle by what they publish and the pictures they print. For example, sometimes gay newspapers and magazines print pictures of drag queens or men with make-up packed on their faces, with pearl necklaces dangling from side to side and with long earrings, wearing pants three sizes too small and cut off at the crotch, area or women walking around bare breasted—signifying that is the image of gay America. Sadly, that is what non-gay media and non-gay people conform to and are directly encouraged to believe is the gay lifestyle. But that's far from being the complete truth; for some, maybe, however for most that behavior is unacceptable.

In contrast, what the public never sees are the lesbians who are the power brokers of their own corporations or the professionals who work in Fortune 500 companies—they are very successful and gay. Nor does the public get the opportunity to observe the gay parents raising their children in a loving environment, fulfilling their responsibilities so well that they blend into the fabric of America. Nor does the image surface of gays and lesbians as proud, hardworking and productive members of society—this wholeheartedly includes the United States military.

To solve this problem, the gay media and gay people must police their own news, and their own actions. The non-gay media must be more sensitive to gay lifestyles. It is noted that people have the freedom to display themselves in any fashion, but to do so doesn't help the gay movement—which is working hard to ensure that gays can be treated with respect and accepted in America as people who live a good alternative lifestyle. People must understand that tolerance is not enough, but acceptance is enough; because,as the world changes, people must learn to accept changes, or things that are different from what they believe.

In the middle of struggling for gay rights, the media seems to forget that the image of the rainbow for gay people is love and unity among brothers and sisters—this issue seems to get lost or is downplayed in the public. Why? The answer reverts back to a passage in chapter one: people seem to care more about what's going on in other people's bedrooms than the state of affairs of the world around them. It does not matter what goes on behind closed doors between consenting adults, specifically when the situation does not affect you directly.

Moreover, the uncommitted individuals who remain on the side of enmity should foster the colors of the rainbow as a symbol of love, unity and freedom. Finally, you are encouraged to begin manufacturing love, acceptance, and togetherness for all people. Attempt to do this regardless of anyone's lifestyle. And most of all, learn to accept change. Change to some is like driving a car in a metropolitan city during rush hour traffic—you are driving along, then you come to a stop, then you creep at a low speed for a few minutes, then you gain speed, then you creep, then stop and go, stop and go; however, if you are patient and keep moving, eventually you will reach your destination. You have to be patient, endure and keep moving....

*IF YOU WANT A PERSON'S BEHAVIOR TO CHANGE THEN CHANGE YOUR BEHAVIOR FIRST.*

—*Melvin Murphy*

## RACE RELATIONS

America still has a serious problem.

It's a problem that is continuing to destroy the fruits and labor of a nation that has spent hundreds of years fertilizing its soil with freedom, equal justice, the pursuit of equality and happiness. It's a solemn problem that has damaged and lengthened the gap between some people in the United States—this being the somber problem of racism.

We are going into the twenty-first century with no plans on improving race relations. What are we going to do to make the world a better place? This current impasse on racism cannot be allowed to continue. In the words of Nobel Laureate Elie Wiesel, we must "aim at preventing future generations from inheriting our past as their future." We must solve this problem right now. However, before we can attempt to solve any problems, we must first define racism and prejudice.

What is prejudice? Prejudice is unfavorable conclusions or opinions formed beforehand, without knowledge; or to judge prematurely and irrationally—to bias. This definition can best be explained by saying prejudice is judging a book by its cover. For example, if there are four caucasian teenagers, two with blond hair, one with red hair, and the fourth with brown hair, riding around in a nice convertible car, having a good time, being wild, loud, laughing and just being all-American boys—it is perceived that they are simply all-American boys having a good time. On the other hand, if there are four African-American teenagers, all with black hair, riding around in the same kind of convertible car, having a good time, being wild, loud, laughing and just being all-American boys—it is often perceived as "Here comes trouble"—that is prematurely judging someone.

Prejudice practiced in America turns to racism. Undoubtedly, this is because of hatred. Racists hate because of fear of cultural, racial or religious differences. In recent years there has been heightened controversy between Jewish Americans and African-Americans. There has been equal name-calling and finger-pointing from people on both sides. Individuals are purposely attempting to destroy the table of brotherhood between the two groups. Why? The answer to this question can be summed up by saying it's for fear of difference. Many people feel they may lose something. Sometimes it is extremely difficult to explain this reasoning—but the bottom line is, we all desire the same things that life has to offer, such as good employment opportunities, a good education for our children, and peace in our communities.

Moreover, it doesn't matter how much a person attempts to wreck the relationship between the Jewish Americans and African Americans, it shall never, never, never be accomplished—the African and Jewish Americans are here to stay; so we'd better learn to live together, and instead of bickering, place the energy into building a stronger country for future generations. Let's start by electing leaders who are not afraid to be leaders. Let's support the leaders who are not afraid to stand up and speak out on all issues—not just the issues they are comfortable in speaking out on. The message is we can fight one another, call each other names, or even hate each other—it's not going to be productive for anyone; so let's bring charity, encouragement, sincerity, love, forgiveness, humility and truth together and build rather than permit malice, discouragement, insincerity, hate, unmercifulness, haughtiness, and falsehood to tear down and force separation.

You can stop racism by washing hatred out of your hair with your personal shampoo—in other words, clean your mind by finding new ways of thinking. Don't be quick to judge someone, and do think positive thoughts of others. While blow-drying or towel drying your hair, wipe or blow away the pain caused by racism.

The pain of feeling emotionally devalued. No matter how hard minority people work and try to do the right things to be productive, they are still discounted because of the color of their skin. Shave bigotry from your face with each stroke of the razor blade—don't wear hate on your face. With each stroke of the toothbrush across your teeth and on your tongue, brush away injurious language.

When all abstract exfoliation has been done, place love on your face as the foundation of make-up. Condition your hair with love and compassion. Smooth your face with acceptance as an after-shave lotion. Mousse, spray, or groom your hair with persistence. Remain steadfast while making sure racism vanishes—just as when hair spray is placed on your hair, it remains stiff and in place—don't be flexible with racism. Gargle with kind words, speak with gentle words. If you do not have something friendly to say, say nothing at all.

Once we have abstractly exfoliated ourselves with this method, we will look and smell fresh—just as when we hang clothing on the outside clothesline to get fresh air. If you can't seem to conceptually exfoliate, then dress your racism in store bought clothing—that will have to be changed the next day. It's up to you to change your behavior and find a new way of thinking.

In your new way of thinking implant permanently in your subconscious mind the need to regularly look beyond the faults and failures of people and see the need. The need to be American citizens who have been given the rights to rise as far as their talents and education can take them, without having the winds of change, strong as a tornado, crash through and destroy their house of hope. Everyone has the right to flourish and be fruitful on their own merits without having external influences such as racism obstruct their progress.

How do we begin to solve the problem of racism in America? Sometimes in life we have to take a stand on issues we believe in with conviction and earnestness; even if the outcome doesn't benefit us directly. Often, people are afraid to stand up for what is right—because of pressures they place on themselves, such as trying to please friends and family. When a person is faced with an unethical racial situation or conversation, instead of taking a position for what is morally right and asking the offender to desist, they may choose to join in—to look as if they are a part of the group--or remain completely silent. Either choice is wrong for different reasons.

The first choice is unfair to the person being ridiculed. Second, it's ethically wrong because the person who could have stopped it remained silent—and silence, according to United States' law, is acceptance. Don't be afraid to stand up for what is just, for yourself and others—whether you agree or not with this principle. Heroes are born through ethical persuasion, and while you may not become a hero, your conscience will be clear if you stand up for what is right and just.

To begin to solve the problem of racism in America, start with yourself. If you were given a firm foundation of what is right and wrong in childhood as, and still practice what you were taught, then you are well on your way to helping others gain awareness of the race problems in America. First, to help eliminate the problem of racism, you must start to re-learn who you are as a person and become secure in the fact that you like yourself—it's called self-confidence. It's having the confidence to stand up for what is right, when others have turned their backs on what is wrong.

Second, we need to provide education about each other's customs and cultures. Since America is a salad bowl of many nationalities, educating people on the various customs and cultures can be an advantage to all people. Also, this will allow the non-American born to preserve their heritage, because "if you give up your heritage to get where you're going, you'll be nothing when you get there." We don't want anyone to feel like nothing in America.

Third, we must focus on the deteriorating conditions of our communities and our great country. America is the greatest country on earth—yes, we have our problems, but where else can you achieve or have anything your heart desires—like freedom of religion, speech and all the other civil rights? We must clean our inner-cities and provide for our youth on a national level.

The United States Government has a sufficient amount of money to do what is needed to accomplish this by educating the public on the worthlessness and destruction that racism creates. On the other side of this coin, American citizens must aid the U. S. Government through volunteering their services.

Finally, we must elect leaders who can lead by motivating.Elect leaders who can motivate our children and others to stay in school, off drugs, and to put down the guns. We must elect leaders that we can look up to, instead of idolizing fictional characters on the television and movie screens. We need leaders—this includes parents and guardians who can be the eyes of the eagle—who can sit high, look low, take charge, and monitor good and bad situations properly.

Often, during a city, state or congressional election, we are able to see the candidates. They come to local events and you are able talk with them; but as soon as the election is over and the winner takes office, you will be lucky if you can get an appointment. On the other hand, they may be too busy doing the jobs they were elected to do.

We do not want leaders to sit in their nice offices and work on surface issues, we need them to get to the grassroots on issues like racism and crime in America. There's still a racism problem in America. Let's hope that the uninformed individuals will become aware of this problem and begin to take a stand against this deadly disease. Let's hope that, as Americans, we can begin to unite and communicate with each other constructively. And when we facilitate this evolution in our lives, and in our children's lives, we will be able to watch many hearts unfold like flowers through the window of hope.

*BEFORE YOU CAN TAKE CARE OF OTHERS...
YOU MUST FIRST TAKE CARE OF YOURSELF.*

*TO UNDERSTAND THE WORLD AND ITS PROBLEMS...
FIRST UNDERSTAND YOURSELF.*

—Melvin Murphy

## DESIRES FOR PEACE

There are many categories for peace. There's peace in ecology and justice. There's desire for peace in third world civil wars and revolutions. There's desire for peace in domestic violence and social change.

All of these categories of peace play a major role in survival for freedom. It is apparent from the world situation that many people desire peace worldwide and some have expired trying to achieve it. The categories mentioned initially are serious crusades; and we hope that the brothers and sisters on the front lines worldwide accomplish their goals in the name of those who have fallen.

What is peace? Peace is living in harmony, with the absence of hostility and physical confrontation--that's why our laws were created, to achieve harmony among people—although it seems something went wrong. Keep in mind that the peace can mean different things to different people.

In this section, the focus is on two kinds of peace: peace of mind and self-realization. Many people have desires for peace but they do not know how to obtain it or where to begin looking for it. Most do not attempt to discover peace, or it's never been a major issue or problem in their everyday lives. Some people would not recognize peace, through no fault of their own, because they are constantly surrounded by disorder.

How does a person find peace? A person must search for harmony by looking in the mirror first. Look within the person who's looking in the mirror—in other words, start with yourself. Starting with yourself is the preparation to finding inner peace. Once you have found harmony within yourself, it will automatically be displayed towards others automatically. Finding inner peace is not a clear-cut process. It is a process that evolves from the things that you do. Inner peace is found by taking better care of yourself. It's found by having self-awareness or an understanding of what makes you genuinely happy. Inner peace can be found by taking better care of yourself through a proper diet, eating healthier, and getting plenty of exercise—exercising makes you feel good physically and mentally.

Inner peace is found by being in control of those circumstances that are controllable, without causing great levels of anxiety in your life. For example, in a car the driver is the controller, the driver says when to stop or when to go, when to turn right or left. There's security in knowing that the driver is in command; but if the car doesn't have brakes, the driver is not in control and that would create a stressful moment. Always have the security of knowing which circumstances you are in control of in your life. If it's an unpleasant situation, you still have the control whether to allow it to affect you or not. This is called self-realization.

**SELF-REALIZATION.**

Self-realization is merely having awareness or an understanding of one's self. To achieve inner peace, we must set goals for ourselves—goals like earning more income, starting a business, building more or stronger friendships or completing a major project. You must set realistic goals, goals that are attainable. Do not set goals that you will not achieve.

Also, to achieve inner peace, you must be honest and confident with yourself as a person. How do you know you're being honest with yourself? Maybe because you're at peace with yourself.

**PEACE OF MIND**

To have peace of mind is to be calm or tranquil within yourself. Peace of mind is found when you choose to take care of your responsibilities because you want to and have the means to do so—not because you have to. Peace of mind is established when the lack of fury and the presence of love represented within yourself and toward your loved ones. Peace of mind can only be found within each person and by each person who desires serenity.

Finding inner peace can be a complicated process. Some people find inner peace and peace of mind through spirituality and religion. Others search for peace through awareness. And those not sure of how to find peace—they shouldn't worry, because people will always be searching for the answer to "How do we find inner peace?

WITH THE RIGHT PEOPLE

IN YOUR LIFE,

YOU CAN ACCOMPLISH

ANYTHING

-MELVIN E. MURPHY

*MOTIVATION IS BEHAVIOR THAT CONTROLS YOUR PERFORMANCE.*

—Melvin Murphy

## MOTIVATION

What is motivation? Motivation is an emotional need to inspire action. Motivation refers to the power of an acquired passion to encourage a certain kind of performance, primarily accomplishing certain goals, achieving occupational success, completing a project, cleaning the house or finding inner peace. Motivation can also be represented by the term "desire." The results they both produce can be paralleled. Mortimer J. Adler said, " when we turn from the realm of thought and theory to the realm of action and the practice, it is our appetites or desires that move or motivate us" to take action. Motivation gives each of us the aspiration to reach our full potential in all that we desire to accomplish. People have diverse needs, attitudes, expectations and dreams—but one thing we all have in common motivation and or the desire within us to achieve our dreams.

What motivates people to succeed?

People are motivated to succeed because of the rewards that they receive upon being successful at their endeavor. The rewards can vary from being satisfied in completing a small project to building a major corporation. For example, people are habitually motivated to work for money or for what money can do—provide a roof over your head; feed a habit we've all grown accustomed to—eating; or allowing the simple pleasures such as dining out, going to a movie, or going shopping to be a part of your life. Others are motivated because of the achievement they feel when helping others—volunteering and assisting in the community.

Everyone has reasons or motives for doing the things they set out to accomplish; whether they're good or not so good, there will be motives. Several basic reasons or motives will incite a reaction in self-performance. They are:

- **Sex**
- **Honor**
- **Passion**
- **Freedom**
- **Ingenuity**
- **Trepidation**
- **Economic Growth**
- **Self-Preservation**
- **Sense of Contribution**
- **Prominence and Power**
- **Fury and Retaliation**

Within these reasons, you will discover what justifies our pursuit to achieve our aspirations. Moreover, people always have reasons to be motivated—just as we all have reasons to be unmotivated. People who are highly motivated often show their motivation outwardly, like the United States Marine who has had a good morning of physical training (better known as PT) and has received a pay check on the fifteenth of the month—now that's motivation. People who are unmotivated also show their behavior outwardly, by being lazy, sluggish, or by how they go about trying to achieve their desires—by talking about it all the time and taking no action to make it become a reality.

In addition, people have a need for others to motivate them. Many times close friends and relatives can inspire an individual to feel good about themselves or encourage them to take action for whatever they desire. Motivation is an individual behavior within each of us—no one can tell us what or how to feel at any point in our lives. Others can only encourage us to take action by what they say and do; which is a good thing, because sometimes we need the support—that's if they provide a positive support system.

For example, there was a woman sixteen year old named Linda with a bright future who was being raised with four siblings by her ailing mother. Unfortunately, her mother passed away, sending Linda's life into a state of confusion—this is to be expected at the age of sixteen. However, Linda never came out of the state of confusion—in fact her condition deteriorated.

A year later, Linda dropped out of high school and began roaming the streets of the city. She stayed out half the night and slept most of the day. Finally, realizing her potential, Linda fought to turn her life around. She joined the Job Corps and went out West for training. But Linda never completed the Job Corps training and returned home.

With the support of family and friends, Linda returned to high school and passed the General Equivalence Degree examination. Unfortunately, Linda fell back into the same lifestyle she'd fought to leave, only this time her life would be changed forever. While she was proud of her GED accomplishment which boosted her confidence and self-esteem, she was also troubled because she had become pregnant and had no financial support or medical coverage.

Nine months later, Linda had a baby girl. Six months after that, Linda again began to take control of her life. She enlisted in the United States Army and served four years. After her enlistment was up, friends and family welcomed her back home. But after a few months at home, with no employment, Linda fell back into the same old lifestyle, and found herself pregnant two more times.

From this point on, a family member had guardianship over Linda's daughter. Linda secured a position at an area mini-market, supporting herself and the two younger children on her salary and government assistance. Linda lived in a trailer park and embraced the same old lifestyle. Ten years would pass before all of the encouragement and support Linda had been given would sink into her mind. Her support system finally worked in her favor; moreover, she began to believe in herself. Linda enrolled in a community college nursing program and graduated three years later.

The message illustrated here is, no matter what kind of trials and hardships you encounter, only you have the motivation to succeed. It may take years as it did with Linda; but remember, her reasons and support systems finally motivated her to succeed. Linda is now a nurse and lives in Texas with her family.

### Establishing High Employee Performance

To get the most productivity from new employees is the prime responsibility of a company and its hiring authorities. When an individual is newly employed, they are excited and eager to impress their new boss and co-workers—not to mention feeling pressured by being closely watched by everyone. Because of this, the new employee isn't thinking of learning their job in depth, their only concern is pleasing management and closely associated co-workers by completing the work that is placed in front of them which can be a mistake.

It is the company and management's responsibility to obtain high performance from new employees. To gain high performance from the start, employers should follow these steps:

**STEP ONE:**

Make absolutely sure the candidate is qualified for the position for which they have applied. Often, companies are under pressure to hire; they may fear losing a contract bid, or need to replace employees who have quit without notice, or have to fill an important slot prior to an expected termination—this causes employers to rush through the hiring process, and the only person that loses in the long run is the new hire. The hiring authorities should without doubt do their homework when it comes to hiring new employees. Make the interview an even exchange of in-depth information, and include information on what to expect on the job.

**STEP TWO:**

Once step one has been executed successfully and the employee is ready to begin training, it is now up to the company and its management to make high performance happen. This step is critical to the success of the individual and the company in the long run. At this stage, management must provide proper and adequate structural training for the new hire. If the position requires on-the-job training, a written training plan should be established.

**STEP THREE:**

Assign a competent trainer for three to six months or the length of the probationary period. This will allow consistent guidance and permit the new hire to see how procedures are performed. This will also provide the new employee with feedback and foster management intervention on how things should be done.

**STEP FOUR:**

Evaluate the performance of the employee before the end of the probationary period. Management must provide feedback directly to the employee.

**STEP FIVE:**

The probation/training period is over. Allow the employee to fly solo. It is a good idea to have a monitoring system in place so the new hire may have assistance when needed. Make sure the monitoring system includes different trainers or employees—this allows the employee to see a variety of acceptable techniques.

These steps can be a guide to eliminating potential performance problems at the start of an employee's career. This will also provide a great level of confidence. When you are confident, it eliminates worries of failure and other problems while arousing a great feeling of self-fulfillment.

Employee Motivation

It takes more than money to keep employees motivated.

# 54   Desire: The Emotional Appetite for Success

Money is no longer a controlling motivator in corporations. Employees require recognition and praise, career advancement, job security, and two-way communication. Let's briefly discuss these requirements:

## Recognition and Praise

This is a major requirement. When people are recognized by management, they feel a sense of pride and self-respect. When management gives praise, it demonstrates their appreciation for the employee's performance. Whether people show it or not, everyone loves to feel appreciated for the work they do.

## Job Security

Job security as it was once known is virtually non-existent today. With a mediocre economy and corporate downsizing, no one has a secure job. Many people have left large companies to start their own businesses due to a lack of job security—but there are still no guarantees of security. The best thing to do is save a "nest egg" for a rainy day.

## Career Advancement

Career advancement is very important to people. Advancing in a career gives the employee a feeling of achievement and accomplishment. The worst thing that can happen to an employee is to be trapped in the same position for an extended period of time while being dissatisfied. This will cause negative feelings that will be reflected in the employee's performance.

## Communication

Communications. It is important that companies have employee problem-solving groups. Establishing a problem solving group will allow individuals to solve certain problems or to reach decisions on specific non-management issues. Also, having this group will increase employee motivation. Because this will build comradardery.

## Organizational Communication

It is essential for corporations to maintain formal employee communications. Organizational communication refers to the messages sent and received within an organization. As corporations become more complex, company communications become more important.

## Intercultural Communication

Intercultural communication has become a major issue today. It refers to communication between individuals who have diverse beliefs and values. This area of communication should be addressed at all levels in any corporation because a lack of knowledge can be devastating to the morale of employees.

Having round table or feedback sessions is a plus for any company. This will allow employees to express their concerns as well as provide suggestions on production improvements within the company. Also, this will give the employee the sense of being a team member and it shows the company cares. Employee communication is vital to all companies and should be practiced at all times.

**Please complete the statements below to give yourself a better perspective of what is needed to achieve your goals. Be specific. Once you have completed the work sheet, then take action.**

*If I had my greatest desire I would:*

_____
_____
_____

*My life would be more satisfying if:*

_____
_____
_____

*My favorite pastime is:*

_____
_____
_____

*I am motivated by:*

_____
_____
_____

*Steps I can take to follow my dreams:*
___
___
___

*It sure would be fantastic if:*
___
___
___

*I need to change these things in my life in order to be successful:*
___
___
___

*I will change my situation by doing:*
___
___
___

*Motivation...is your food for success.*

*Motivation...keeps you believing.*

—Melvin Murphy

## Staying Motivated

Staying motivated can be a problem when you are trying to achieve success. At times you can feel quite lonely when starting any business venture—because all of the responsibilities fall on your shoulders. You may feel skeptical about the decisions you have made and fear failure in the back of your mind. To keep yourself motivated, you must think of the wonderful outcome in being successful.

Staying motivated is a large piece of the puzzle in being successful. Staying motivated is usually like putting gasoline into your car—the more gasoline you have, the longer your car will run. In other words, if you stay motivated in your endeavors, the chances of fulfilling your dreams will increase. They will increase because you now have the fuel it will take to reach your destination; if not, then you will have to re-fuel.

If you allow your car, to run out of gasoline, it will sit in that same spot until it is towed or until you put more fuel in the gas tank. Similarly, if you allow yourself to run out of motivation, your endeavors or dreams will sit in the same spot where you ran out of motivation. Here are several principles to help you stay motivated:

1. *Make a commitment to your endeavor.* You must be dedicated to yourself and to your quest. You must live your dreams with devotion at all times.

2. *Surround yourself with good people.* Surrounding yourself with people who will help broaden your perspective provides an added benefit. Surround yourself with mentors who do not mind sharing their knowledge openly and completely. You must research great people in your chosen field and find out what it was that made them achieve greatness.

3. *Have a positive mental attitude.* For instance, while vacationing in Saint Thomas, Virgin Islands, I met a restaurant waitress with a positive mental attitude that should be bottled and sold. (Let's call her Randi.) Randi was in her late fifties, possibly early sixties. What was atypical about Randi was that, she had on beautiful diamonds from head to ankles. Now, I realize that waitresses do not make grand salaries; yet, Randi had beautiful diamonds that resembled bright miniature light bulbs. She had diamonds in her earlobes, around her neck, on both wrists, on several fingers, and around her ankles. With her lovely personality , she engaged us in conversation, as we were the only customers in the restaurant for lunch. Through the joking and laughing, the question was asked, how could Randi afford beautiful diamonds working as a waitress? Her response made all the sense in the world. She said, "I can afford anything through hard work and a positive attitude." She went on to say, "You only live once. If you want it, get it, because you can't take it with you when you die. The only thing you will take with you when you die is the food in your stomach, so you have to work for what you want." The table fell silent and all eyes and ears were intently focused on Randi. We learned a valuable lesson that day and spent lots of money in the remaining vacation days. The lesson we learned was that you must have a positive mental attitude for what you want and be prepared to work to attain it.

4. *Employ the knowledge, help and influence of your friends.* Everyone knows someone who has connections—in other words, "network." A word of caution: be particular in the friends you choose.

5. *Don't be afraid of going after your dream.* If you work hard enough you'll get what you wish for. Don't back out when the ball begins to roll—this is the moment you have been waiting for. Go ahead with full strength.

6. *Believe in yourself when others don't.* Believe you will succeed in your endeavors. For example, if you have fifty

people believing the answer to a question is no, and you believe within your heart the answer is yes, stand by your belief because the other forty-nine people could be wrong. Have conviction and listen to your inner voice.

7. *Take charge and remain in control.* For instance, if you've ever watered a lawn while holding a water hose, you know that the hose has pressure when the water is on. If you let go of the hose, it will whip around in all directions, spraying water everywhere, but if you hold onto the hose the water spray remains controlled. Always have control in your business. Also, remain in control by signing your own business or personal checks.

8. *Have a good support system in place.* This is very important. You want to be around people who will encourage you and give you impetus. You want to be around people who are doing what you are doing.

9. *Always have direction.* A lack of direction will cause problems. Case in point: When you mail a letter and forget to put the zip code on the envelope, you might get lucky and find that the post office will continue to process your letter to the proper destination. But, if you forget to put the address on the envelope your mail will be returned to you. The message here is, when you mail a letter you give the post office directions. You know what it will take to get your letter to the desired destination and what the post office needs to assist you. Now give yourself direction so that you know how to complete your objectives and get to the point which you desire.

10. *Visualize and act out your dreams.* Visualizing your dreams will give you a mental picture of where you want to be and what you want to do. Acting out your dreams will place you in the position of being what you want to be. For example, when you are at a private party or having a conversation, the question of your line of work will usually come up. If you are in the beginning stages of starting a home bakery and you also work for another company as a receptionist, when you are asked about your

line of work, simply say, "I am a baker, here's my card." The downside of this is, you must have enough knowledge about the profession to carry on a conversation—in addition, you should know enough to carry on a conversation with another baker or person in the profession.

11. *Use your creative imagination to achieve your dreams.* Everyone could be doing what you are doing. You must create a unique way of achieving your goals. Research your field and discover how others completed their goals—then dissect the procedures and find a way to make them better.

You have the power within you to achieve all of your desires. You must make a solid commitment to be devoted to your endeavors. You have the power to find good mentors to train you and the power to realize whether your support system is an advantage or disadvantage in your quest. Ultimately, you have the power to employ the knowledge necessary to achieve success.

You have the power to believe in yourself and take control. The power is within you to maintain proper direction without fear. You possess the power to be creative and utilize all of the personal techniques to make you feel like or become a member of the profession you seek. The motivational power is within you to achieve success.

## WATCHING OTHERS SUCCEED.

Watching others succeed can be depressing or it can be impressing. Watching others succeed can be depressing because you want that same success to happen to you. It's depressing because it looks so easy when you see someone else achieving what you want to achieve. It's depressing because you feel you do not have the self-confidence, motivation, or determination to endure the battles it will take to reach the pinnacle.

It's depressing because you feel you have the persistence, drive, and belief to fight the necessary battles to reach your goals, and yet you're not getting anywhere. It's depressing because you are putting in the extended work hours, but it just doesn't seem to be happening for you.

Why not? This question can only be answered by you. You must retrace, go over, or reevaluate your plan of action. If you have completed the troubleshooting and the diagnostics check out, but a problem remains, do as IBM (International Business Machines) Customer Engineers do when trying to fix a computer problem: swap parts until you fix the problem. Your plan is as "strong as its weakest link."

It's depressing because you can't seem to locate the problem on paper. If the problem isn't in the plan of action or the work hours—because you have dug in and have given your all—then what is it? The problem must be in your heart. The problem is in your heart because you have allowed jealousy over other people's successes to stand in your way. The problem is in your heart because you have allowed envy to cloud your thinking—you should be thinking "there's enough success out there for everybody, and if others can do it, so can I." This is a natural feeling because you want the same success and wonder why you have not received it. But you must be HUNGRY for success. You must be STARVING for success, regardless of what you see others doing in their quest.

Watching others succeed can be impressive because it empowers you to know success can be yours. It's impressive because if you have the belief, appetite, and persistence to weather the storms, you will achieve the same level of success as the others.

It's impressive because it's a matter of time before the stormy weather is over—it doesn't always rain. It's impressive because you realize what kind of person you must become to reach your goals. It's impressive because the long hours you've worked will be rewarded in the end. It's impressive because it is not over until you win....

And how do you win? You will win by staying hungry. You must have a desire to be successful or you wouldn't be reading this motivational book—in abstract, this motivational book is like a gourmet feast exquisitely prepared and served on a plate.

You will not be forced, ordered, or implored to eat this elegantly prepared feast served on your plate. However, if you are hungry enough for success, you will eat and digest this wonderful experience that has been prepared just for you.

You must go after your dreams as if you are searching for food on a deserted island. (Being emotionally hungry is discussed in Ch. 4.) You must choose a meal that will ultimately satisfy your hunger. Finally, only you know if the main course is what you desire. "Bon appetit."

### Here are ten affirmations to recite daily.

1. I am the secret ingredient in all that I make happen.

2. I think I can, I think I can, and I will.

3. I will take action to make things happen in my life.

4. I have the desire, the emotional appetite for my success.

5. I will become successful by helping myself and others.

6. I will break my glass circle to reach my desire by working diligently and believing.

7. I can achieve, because I believe.

8. I will learn my craft to perfection.

9. Everyday I will fulfill one objective toward my goal.

10. My motivation is my fuel for optimum performance and sustained energy for mind power.

—Melvin Murphy

*CLUBS AND ORGANIZATIONS CAN PRODUCE ENERGY AND PUSH YOU TO NEW HEIGHTS.*

—*Melvin Murphy*

## CLUBS, ORGANIZATIONS AND GOOD PEOPLE

Belonging to clubs, associations, and organizations with good people is an essential part of the process in being successful in your career. It is essential to belong to clubs or associations because they provide valuable information about your profession. It is essential to be a member of associations because they provide you with guidelines and proper protocol for your industry. It is essential to belong to clubs or associations because it grants the opportunity to meet top professionals in your field, and your membership will provide a great opportunity to network among your industry peers.

Being a club or association member means you belong to an organized group of people who meet regularly for a specific purpose. Being an organized entity gives a group of people the alliances necessary to make a difference in their industry, and belonging to such an organization will provide new professionals with career assistance. Being in a well-organized association or club can make a significant difference in your career—it can mean the difference between success and failure.

Case in point: when I was an up-and-coming motivational speaker, I had a message I believed the world needed to hear. I didn't exactly know how I would get my message out to the world, so I began searching for speaking organizations that could help me. I eventually came across an organization known for training people to enhance their speaking abilities.

This organization is called Toastmasters International. Toastmasters International is a nonprofit organization designed to help people enhance their speaking abilities by providing structural self-paced training. I joined a local Toastmasters club's that met on Saturday mornings at eight o'clock. The Toastmasters club name is G. U. T. S.—Get Up To Speak. Eight o'clock is awfully early on a Saturday morning—it takes guts to get up early on a Saturday when you do not have to.

Through my love and dedication for this club, I would fight Mr. Sleep every Saturday morning to be at this meeting so I could have a chance to speak. (In any Toastmasters club meeting, coming to a meeting and not talking is completely unacceptable—you are asked to say a few words, even if it's your first time.) During my tenure in the G. U. T. S. club, I competed in speech contests in and outside the club, placing first or second in all contests. I became known to club members for delivering powerful Saturday morning speeches. I eventually developed a reputation around the Washington, D. C., area for wanting to speak at any Toastmasters club. After a year and a half, I was awarded my Competent Toastmaster award. This award is the first of many given to individuals who have met certain requirements of successful course completion and have developed their skills in the art of public speaking.

Belonging to the Toastmasters organization afforded me the opportunity to develop, learn, and grow in the art of public speaking. The Toastmasters organization has given me the opportunity to meet and learn from good people who train new toastmasters as a hobby because they love to use the natural instrument that has been bestowed upon them.

Becoming a member of a specific organization or association is also beneficial because you may receive benefits such as discounted industry insurance, low-cost seminars and conferences, opportunities for improved income, and much more. As a member, you receive industry publications, which keep you informed. Becoming a member of your industry association not only provides support and motivation but exposes you to good people who are trying to achieve the same goals you are attempting to achieve. You also surround yourself with people who have experience and will give you guidance so you will not encounter the same pitfalls as they did when they started.

Having a membership in any organization comes with its responsibilities. Each member is responsible for attending regular meetings, being supportive of officers and all club decisions, and most importantly, paying membership dues on time.

Having good people in your corner is a plus. Associating with good people in your organization is a plus because you can find mentors—people who are willing to provide you with guidance to be successful in your career. Having a mentor is important because your mentor can introduce you to people who are already successful in your profession. If the person you choose has a respectable reputation, their introduction will give you credibility. If their reputation is not so good, then your credibility will not be so good either. Choose your mentor carefully. Remember, a mentor will often choose you—but you still need to be careful.

Not every person who decides to help you is a mentor. Some people will feed you bits and pieces of information because they fear you will succeed beyond what they have achieved; this kind of person you do not want to be involved with at all. Some people will seek to gain information from you and even steal your ideas and put them into action for themselves. Be careful and limit the amount of information you give to people you do not know—remember, not everyone is as ethical as you are.

Then there are people who will see your earnestness and desires, to achieve and they will give you all of the assistance you need without having a hidden agenda of their own. Case in point: as an up and coming motivational speaker, I attended a conference of the National Speakers Association. With events going on every minute, we were all exhausted by the end of the day. It turned out to be the toughest week I ever loved and it was there that I met the person I would come to trust for guidance. Even though this person lives in Columbus, Ohio, we are frequently in communication with each other.

This person took me under his wing and instantly began providing me with valuable information about our industry. I was able to recognize the sincerity in the help I was getting and communicated my appreciation to the person, thus opening the doors to developing a good relationship. The type of person who will take you under his or her wing is going beyond the call of duty because they want to. This is the type of person you want to be associated with and have as a mentor. This person will help you mature greatly in your profession.

To be sure you have chosen a good mentor, evaluate the person by what they do and say to you. For example, when I was into martial arts, I had dreams of opening a martial arts school. I wanted to open a school because I felt I could provide a good service. I felt confident in my abilities, for I had been trained by one of the best instructors in the business. I had grown to admire, trust, and respect my martial arts instructor.

When I decided to actively pursue this dream, I confided in my instructor—I told him all of my plans explicitly, and sought his trusted advice on issues. Once I had secured financing for my project, I began looking for a suitable location. Being a small fish in a big sea, there were certain places I could not afford to lease, making my search difficult. I spent a year searching and negotiating with commercial realtors.

Finally, when I found a location and began to contact the renters, I unexpectedly began seeing advertisements in the newspaper for a martial arts school coming to the surrounding area. A friend and I began figuring out the whereabouts of this new school. Weeks later, the grand opening for this martial arts school came. I had planned to investigate the competition the day of its opening but failed to do so, but my friend who lived in the area did go. He returned home only to call me bearing bad news that he knew would devastate me, and had upset him as well.

My friend said, "Melvin, I went to the new school we talked about, and guess what? It's nice, real nice. My heart stopped for what seemed like a minute. He went on to say, "But I have to tell you something else. Guess who was there?" I began guessing and was wrong on every guess. He said, "I saw this familiar face and said 'I know him!' Then, he said, someone mentioned the man's name. It was my instructor.

I was devastated. After I got off the telephone, I began to clean out my office full of martial arts supplies that I had planned to utilize for my own opening. In the middle of this clean up, I sat down in the middle of the floor and cried. I cried because the person I had trusted and respected for seven had years betrayed me in two ways. First, he stabbed me in the back by opening a martial school in the location I had selected, and second, he didn't even ask me to be his partner. I guess my money and talent weren't good enough—so I thought. (At press time for this book, I still haven't talked with my former instructor.)

Although he owed me no explanation, my instructor once again taught me a valuable lesson. He taught me that 1) some people are determined to succeed no matter who they deceive, and 2) not to just look, but to see from now on—this means, like the old saying goes, "all that glitters ain't gold."

In selecting your mentors, choose carefully. Don't forget to open your eyes and see; do not just look. If they are not providing the guidance you seek, do not be afraid to find a new mentor, because it's your career that's at risk, not theirs. Finally, when you do find a good mentor, don't hang on to their every advice blindly; make sure you rationalize all of your decisions before taking any action. Make sure you have made the best decisions for yourself.

At speaking engagements I'm often asked, How do I find an association that's appropriate for me? Start with your local library. There is a book that lists every association in the United States—the book is called *The Encyclopedia of Associations*. This book lists a variety of information such as total number of members, yearly budgets, publications produced, a contact person, address, telephone numbers, and a brief description of the organization's mission. This book will most likely be a reference book and cannot be checked out of the library. Also, you may wish to check with the Chamber of Commerce in your area for a list of local clubs and organizations.

Are associations expensive to join? Most associations are nonprofit organizations, meaning they do not make a profit as a business. In fact, most nonprofit organizations and associations are constantly trying to overcome demanding cashflow problems. Although organizations and associations have membership fees to join, the fees vary from twenty-five dollars to five hundred dollars, depending upon the organization.

When should I join an association? The time to join any association is when you are financially capable. Joining any association is a serious commitment because the existing members will be expecting you to be an active member by participating and volunteering your time to promote and build the organization.It is recommended that you do not join until you have committed yourself to their purpose and are willing to work toward their goals.

Before you decide to join any association/organization, ask yourself these questions:

1. Why do I want to join this association/organization?

2. What do I plan to gain from this association/organization?

3. How will I gain this by joining this association?

4. Do I have the finances to join?

5. Am I willing to commit to volunteering my time to help support the organization?

6. Can this association/organization help me reach my goals?

7. How many times will I attend regular meetings?

8. *What special talents do I have to help the organization?*

_____
_____
_____

*If I join an association or organization, is my membership fee tax-deductible?* The dues for most nonprofit organizations can be a tax deduction if you are self-employed. If you are unsure of your organization's tax status, ask someone or contact the Internal Revenue Service in your city or in Washington, D.C.

Joining associations and organizations will be exciting and fulfilling. But remember, you will only get as much out of the organization as put into it. It is highly recommended that you join your industry association if you plan to climb the ladder of success. Joining your industry association will give you a feeling of belonging, motivation, and a sense of accomplishment. Good luck!

**Association Sources**
1. The Encyclopedia of Associations, Gale Research Company, Detroit, MI, 1-800-877-Gale extension 4000.
2. The National Organizations of the United States (local library).
3. Your local Chambers of Commerce.
4. Your local Better Business Bureau.
5. The Library of Congress, Washington, D. C.
6. Your local library (reference section).
7. The Department of Commerce, Washington, D. C.
8. The telephone book (business section).

Unlock

the great possibilities

in your life

by following

your true

desires

-Melvin E. Murphy

*When you're hungry, you search for food...
Make the same commitment to feed your passion
for the success that you desire.*

—Melvin Murphy

## Desire: The Emotional Appetite For Success

Have you ever wanted something so much, you thought you were going to die if you didn't get it? Or have you ever hoped for something and believed you would get it as a gift, but you never did? What about the time you wanted to win that contest because you knew you were the best and thought you deserved it? Or the time you prayed to your deity to give you strength, wisdom, financial independence, and to help make your career or venture a success? This feeling of wanting can be called desire—an emotional appetite that everyone has and at one time or another has acted upon.

Desire is an emotional hunger that is fed by gaining exactly what you are craving. Being successful in your business, professional, or personal life by earning the amount of money you want, watching your projects come to a successful completion, or being happy in your everyday life with family and friends, occurs from an emotional feeling; which has to be fulfilled. For example, there was a company called Corporate Kicks, Incorporated. The company's objective was to establish martial arts in corporations as a stress reduction and self-defense program. It was founded by a young motivated entrepreneur who found himself experiencing great levels of unhealthy stress and tension on the job; in fact he had a car accident because of the stress. Fortunately, what could have been a serious accident turned out to be minor collision at a traffic light. After the accident, several years passed before the inspiring entrepreneur quit his corporate engineering position with a Fortune 500 company—during the peak of the 1991 recession without having another job lined up. Luckily, a position came open at the martial arts school where he had trained and become highly proficient in the martial arts.

After a few months on his new job, he decided to start Corporate Kicks, Inc., The Joy of Discipline for Business, a fitness program. He made a decision to change his life and a commitment to help others rid stress and tension from their lives and on the job. With an emotional hunger, he began working night and day creating his business plan and programs for the future clients he knew he would accumulate. The business plan and programs took him one year to complete and left him with a twenty thousand dollar deficit, which he paid with paychecks from the martial arts job. After all of the extensive planning, this young man launched a public relations campaign that gained him the best media coverage a new company could get, from Ontario, Canada, to Atlanta, Georgia rom Los Angeles, California, to New York City. He gained his largest client in the Washington, D.C., area.

My hard work, determination, persistence, and emotional hunger pushed me to a successful completion of my desire. Not only desiring to be successful, but taking action, having faith, and unrelenting stick-to-it-iveness produced the outcome I desired. I would later say: "If I had failed, at least I would have learned that I can succeed by attempting to try and by not giving up."

Desire is an emotional thirst that can be quenched with the liquids of attainment that make you feel valued within. For example, anything that makes you feel good within, like having new possessions, peace of mind, or desired success, helps satisfy your thirst and increases your confidence.

Some people can't understand the emotional thirst for success that others possess. Case in point: two young men who were roommates and good friends. We'll call them Doug and Vinny. Doug has a Masters of Business Administration degree (MBA) which he received after going straight through high school, college, and graduate school. Doug is completely satisfied with his career. On the other hand, Vinny is an ambitious young man who was less fortunate in getting a college degree. Unbeknownst to his parents, Vinny enlisted in the military after high school because he felt his family could not afford to have three teenagers in college at the same time. After, Vinny was honorably discharged from the service he began to pursue another career. He then went through the winds of adversity, hard knocks, rocks and changes.

Through his wind and rock expedition, Vinny learned that a hungry attitude would secure him the job he wanted—and it did. Today, Vinny is completing his college degree and is pursuing another career. His good friend Doug will do anything to help Vinny—which is a good friend to have. But, Doug doesn't seem to understand Vinny's appetite for unconventional success—like starting a business. He thinks Vinny should get a job and be satisfied, but Vinny really wants to be in business for himself. In reality, Doug and Vinny have the same passion for dining at the same restaurant, but they are selecting dinner from different menus.

Some people do not understand the emotional thirst of others because they are not thirsty themselves or they can live without achieving unconventional success. Vinny wants his own business because he wants the freedom to be creative. He wants to work hard for himself and reap the rewards that come along with being a successful entrepreneur. He wants the enjoyment of providing a direct service to people. To explain, let's use the analogy of making concentrated orange juice. When a person mixes a twelve ounce can of concentrated orange juice with water, the orange juice is made—a finished product ready to be served. In relation to quenching the emotional thirst, those who are not thirsty just see a finished product of orange juice—what they don't see is the work it has taken to make the orange juice. What they don't see is buying the juice at the store, transporting the juice, mixing the juice, and the appetite for the juice. They don't see the process.

Mostly what people want to see or taste is a finished product or project. In principle, what most people want to see is an individual who will fit in a mold for them, not the mold you have chosen for yourself. The message here is, when others don't understand or choose not to help, you must empathize with their lack of understanding and remember you may have to make the juice alone; if so, look beyond their faults and failures. Eventually, they will come to understand your passion. In understanding this, make your orange juice, regardless of whether you have help or understanding of your emotional thirst for the success you seek.

**THE THREE QUESTIONS.**

*Where have you been? Why are you here? Where are you going?* Each of these questions has desire as a response. Having desire to do, to be, or to go is the initial starting place before we can accomplish any predetermined goals. For example, when you run your Saturday morning errands to the grocery store, post office, bank or whatever the case may be, it is desire that energizes you, followed by action.

Placing action behind your desires is how you will succeed or fail at your goals—nevertheless, you must have action. If your desire and action do not produce your final goal, do not concern yourself about what others will say or what they think—because you have succeeded. You now have something you can take with you to your next undertaking—knowledge.

Following are three questions. Please take a minute to answer these questions openly and completely. These questions will help you see where you have been and where you are planning to go. If you are not satisfied with your answers, it's time to make changes. Think carefully.

1. *Where have you been?*
   _____
   _____

2. *Why?*
   _____
   _____
   _____

3. *Why are you here? (settling instead of doing what you desire)*
   _____
   _____
   _____

# DESIRE: THE EMOTIONAL APPETITE FOR SUCCESS

4. *Has your current situation helped you get to the place you want to be? (If not, why?)*
   _____
   _____
   _____

5. *Where are you going? (your goals)*
   _____
   _____
   _____

6. *How will you achieve this?*
   _____
   _____
   _____

## MURPHY'S LAWS FOR ACHIEVING SUCCESS

**Law one:** *Know what you want.*

**Law two:** *Believe in yourself.*

**Law three:** *Take action.*

**Law four:** *Seek intelligent answers to reach your objectives.*

**Law five:** *Evaluate your progress. (Is your strategy working or not?)*

**Law six:** *Pursue, persist, persevere and never give up.*

**Law seven:** *Anything that happens will happen because you've made it happen.*

**Law eight:** *Be responsible for what you do, make your own decisions.*

**Law nine:** *Learn to motivate yourself in difficult times.*

**Law ten:** *Know what you're worth, before it's too late.*

To conclude this section, I want to tell you about an experience I had at a speaker's conference. The simple act of dining in the company of eight unknown people changed the way I think, my desires, and my emotional appetite for success forever.

It was time to dine and everyone was choosing their table—trying to secure a location with friends, with people they had been trying to speak with for the past twelve hours or people they had met at the conference. This was the only chance to converse with them. This was a five day conference, with events going on every minute of the day—it was the toughest week a speaker could ever love, and the friendliest of people were in attendance. I was the first to sit at this beautifully set dining table at the Washington Hilton in Washington, D. C. Others began arriving at the table and before you knew it, all of the introductions were made, conversations began, and the table was full, except for one chair.

All of a sudden, a young man in a wheelchair was being assisted to the table. This young man was immutably scarred all over his face and hands. A part of his nose had been reconstructed and he virtually had no fingers—it seemed he had been in a fire, but no one was sure of his situation. Every eye at the table focused on him and a silence fell on the table for the first course of the dinner. "Hello everyone, I'm (John Doe)," he said. Everyone returned pleasant salutations.

John placed the cloth napkin in his lap; the bread and butter came, the salad came, more bread came, and finally the entree arrived. I watched John intensely, trying not to be obvious, not realizing that this person sitting beside me who was making me uncomfortable would change my life. Finally, the dessert came, coffee and tea came, and the program was about to start.

Then I realized how remarkable this young man was; I witnessed a man with no fingers place a cloth napkin in his lap, butter his own bread, eat a salad and a five course meal with desert, drink coffee, and not drop a crumb or spill a drop. In fact, I realized that I was making myself uncomfortable. Here I was, sitting and feeling sorry for him, but by the end of dinner, I began feeling sorry for myself and how I had taken life for granted. This young man had obviously made great progress in his life to be able to handle himself the way he did. It was pretty evident his desire to take care of himself outweighed his impairments. I had a clear understanding that if John could achieve the basics of eating without fingers, I could achieve anything that I desired through knowing who I am, my abilities, and what I can accomplish through my emotional appetite for success.

The message in this heartfelt story is, don't take life and the natural elements you have been given—like having fingers, being able to feed yourself, or just being able to walk—for granted.

One day, while walking across the campus of The American University in Washington, D. C., I emerged from a building and saw the most beautiful scene one could imagine. On this particular day I had not read, heard nor seen the weather forecast, so I was completely surprised by the rain dropping like a heavy mist, covering the clean and beautiful campus. This picture was very misleading; although beautiful, the rain was coming down hard enough to wet the backs of pant legs, book bags and anything that was uncovered as you walked. As I began to walk in the rain and focus my eyes, I noticed a young quadriplegic man in a wheelchair who was a struggling to seek shelter from the rain. As he turned the wheels of his wheelchair he was not moving anywhere. Needless to say, I assisted the young man and made a friend. He said, "I love the rain, but my wheels get slippery when it's raining. Thank you for your help."

The point still remains, appreciate and understand who you are and the natural elements you have been given. Know your abilities, and know that if you make the commitment, you can achieve your emotional appetite for success, regardless of any impairment or limitations you may have or the obstacles placed in your path. So remember: anything that doesn't harm you will make you stronger in your *Desire: The Emotional Appetite For Success*.

*Roads from the past can lead to a brighter future.*
—Melvin Murphy

## Facing A New Challenge

We are now entering the doorway to the twenty-first century and we should treasure the privilege to be a part of what will become history to future generations. We enter this new and exciting period filled with love, hope, and great expectations. It is also a period that's filled with uncertainty for what lies ahead. We stand at the threshold between two centuries—the old way we did things and the continuation of the old way we are doing things. Many would agree that the piercing sounds of dissatisfaction from Haiti, the uprisings in Rwanda, the outbreak in Bosnia, the falling brick walls of Russia, and the social problems in America are all ambassadors of a deep-seated and disastrous problem that has encircled our society.

In the past few years, many have come to accept that we are living in a distressing period. We do not want to believe that the world is still full of hatred, discontent, hidden racism and a lack of respect for human life. There are those who refuse to believe the situation has greatly deteriorated. Today, it seems we are regressing to the time of animosity, hostility, and strife towards each other, instead of advancing to attain brotherhood, sisterhood, unity and peace among all people.

There comes a time when people get tired of witnessing the abuse of citizens by officials who are sworn to protect. There comes a time when people get tired of being victims in their own homes, where they are supposed to encounter safety and peace, not the shadows of constant fear—we are no longer free if we live in fear. There comes a time when people get tired of constant violence, hatred, subtle discrimination, racism and plain bigotry. Although we are tired of it all, we must choose to rise up and challenge these man-made violations. We have a government that's run by the people and for the people; we have the capability to produce a strong economic system, and to eliminate poverty; we have a strong educational system and there should not be illiteracy in America—we must control these entities like steering a car. Only by becoming active in the process can the people can tell the government what is to be done.

The American people must break away from being controlled by the criminals, thugs, and bad guys—break away from being afraid to testify in court if a crime has been witnessed; break away from turning our backs on the evils in our communities; break away from gang violence; and break away from being satisfied in situations that are wicked, to being satisfied with what is morally right. The American people must break away from antiquated, archaic and passe ways of thinking about how we live—these are not the good ole days anymore; this is today, and yesterday does not count any longer. We the American people must look through that telescope called tomorrow and see what lies ahead by observing the path we are now on. The American people must move through the wilderness of change toward the meadowlands of acceptance, serenity, tranquility and racial harmony amongst this diverse nation. As we look back and see that the old world of the 70's and 80's has passed away, and the new difficulties of the 90's—gaining freedom from crime, drug wars, unemployment, racial discontentment and disorder of world peace have infiltrated into the American way of life. We should not allow this kind of behavior continue to govern the way we live.

America is a world leader. Why can't she lead in the extermination of racism, drugs, drug wars, and drug lords that are killing or corrupting our innocent children? We must work to allow children to be children once again. We must bring back the power of family. When will America lead in the elimination of senseless crimes against precious human life? It is time for America to exercise its super powers, as it has done in other countries like Kuwait, Iraq and India, by eradicating racial and social discontentment in America. It is time for America to lead by bringing world peace into its own back yard.

While living with these unfortunate circumstances, many Americans have come to the point of losing faith in themselves and the American way of life. They have come to believe that conceivably this is the practice that will remain in our society. The great distress is that it influences people to believe they are helpless and defenseless; they are made to feel as though nothing they do or say is helpful in making positive changes in themselves and in their communities. As long as we remain complacent, quiet and uninvolved, government will contend it's doing the right things while we the American people are dissatisfied.

It has become a fearful satisfaction in which the American people feel obligated to accept violence, injustice, and discontentment. It is a negative satisfaction. Genuine satisfaction is not simply the lack of negative satisfaction—hatred, crime and disorder; it is working toward the presence of positive satisfaction—fairness, good will and peace toward all.

What must influence the American people to rise up and want a positive change? Unsatisfactory circumstances can bring people of all backgrounds, race, color, and creed together and make a positive change for the betterment of our nation and its people. As the late great Rev. Dr. Martin Luther King, Jr. said, *"Nobody is going anywhere, we are all here to stay."* We must acquire a new self-respect and a new sense of honor among all people.

As we face this new challenge, we must accept the responsibilities that come along with it. A new challenge carries with it new difficulties. Let us address some of the new challenges that we are faced with today.

First, we are challenged to grow beyond the boundaries of self-preservation to a global interest of all man and womankind. Facing a new challenge is a mission to bring solidarity of broken worlds together. This means that no one person or nation can act alone. We must all agree to live together, or we will ultimately destroy one another. This new challenge of global togetherness can be brought about to an enormous degree by American education and technological brilliance.

Through education and technology, we will be able to manage our world and replace violence, disruption, and disorder in succession. Through the power of global superhighways, we are able to communicate to others in countries like China, Greece, and India by computers; or we can communicate by next day mail service from New York to Los Angeles. Through education and technology, we have made the world accessible and this makes it possible to approach making peace through worldwide communications.

Through today's technology, education, and desires, we must make the world a global fraternity of brotherhood and sisterhood. All of us can be involved in this complex strategy. Anything that affects one person in our society affects all of us. We are all connected by desires and emotions for compassion to love all mankind, just as we are attached to our wallets and purses and the contents in them—it's our everyday life line.

A second new challenge that we face is achieving excellence in our dreams, goals, and aspirations. With this new challenge, it will be more difficult to gain employment if we have not educated ourselves to the degree that we are able to compete for employment—by continuing with education beyond high school. America has become a salad bowl and competition has become global—in other words, you are not only competing for jobs with citizens of the United States, but with other citizens from other countries. Therefore, we cannot simply be good at our jobs anymore, we must perform the job to the point that no one can perform it better.

Perform your job to the best of your ability so that when you die or leave, you will be remembered as the best ever. Douglas Mallock said, "If you can't be a pine on the top of the hill, be a scrub in the valley—but be the best little scrub by the side of the hill, be a bush if you can't be a tree. If you can't be a highway just be a trail, if you can't be the sun be a star; it isn't by size that you win or fail—be the best of whatever you are," or be the best that you can be at what you do.

Our third challenge stands face to face with us, which is to bring back peace in our communities, take drugs off of our streets, bring complete equality to all people, love for self and love for others. This clearly means that mothers, fathers and guardians must instill the much-needed values of love, compassion and forgiveness—which should become the foundation of family.

There is the jeopardy of those who have lived under the pressures of mistreatment, those who have been manipulated and stepped on or walked over, those who are outraged by the way that society has treated them, and those who will take the challenge with animosity and a hostile attitude.

We must not let animosity and hostility take over our challenge that we need to win; if we allow hostility and animosity to control us, our purpose is destroyed before we attempt to begin. We must not contaminate the future with lethal poison from the past. This is why desire for love and peace is important. Without love and peace nothing will be accomplished. Our actions will only create more adversity. If we do not have love and peace in our quest for positive change, generations of today and generations that precede us will be the recipients of prolonged days of turbulent storms of hatred; and what we create today is what they will receive tomorrow as our gift of tradition.

We have a phenomenal opportunity to change the dimensions of life so that people will regain a sense of respect for human life and practice love and peace toward each other. There are voices crying out that echo within the breath of the nation, saying: Stop the violence, stop the drugs, save our children and love one another. Those are the voices of people who have grown weary and have exhausted every means by every attempt, and have now fallen to their knees and are pleading for love and peace to all generations.

The love and peace will be the rejuvenation of our nation. Through peace we will close the gaps of lost generations and make love. Through love we will make new friends, have extended families and have peace within ourselves and our communities. This cannot be accomplished with hate at the forefront; but only through love. We must remember that the road from the past can lead to a brighter future.

Finally, if we are to face the new challenge, we must have courage to stand up for what is right and speak out against wrongful deeds performed by people in our presence. Whenever we find someone speaking unkindly about someone else, we must have the strength to refrain from joining in. We must have the strength to say, to paraphrase Maya Angelou,

"Not around me you won't," which signifies that she will not allow unkind words to be spoken about anyone around her.

Someone will ask, " How can I help in this new challenge for peace and love among all people?" We must find help in the amazing power of unity and courage that we have stored within the fibers of our minds and bodies. We must make every complication a breakthrough toward our goals of creating love and a much-needed peace in America.

There is nothing in the human race greater than love. It is something that can't be bought with money; it is something that can't be taken for granted; it is something that can't be seen; It is something that is earned; it is something that can be given freely; and most importantly, it is something that we need to feel.

When we unite in doing all of these things we will be able to create a refreshing environment—a new world in which men and women will live in harmony as brothers and sisters; a world in which men and women will utilize their education to be innovative and create new ways to make life better for humanity.

This must become the way of life. Love, peace, and unity must flow as freely as the wind from the Statue of Liberty in New York through the Gateway in Saint Louis, down to the grand canyons in Arizona, and spring up like the Old Faithful geyser in Wyoming. And not only that, let love and peace spread across the silver screens so everyone can see the what they have created. And when they see their beautiful creation, they will be able to say, "Oh, what a beautiful city! Oh, what a beautiful city!"

Please read this poem as food for thought...

### THE MAN IN THE GLASS

*When you get what you want in your struggle for gain*
*And the world makes you king for a day,*
*Just go to the mirror and look at yourself*
*And see what the man has to say!*
*It isn't your father or mother or wife*
*Whose judgment upon you must pass;*
*The one whose verdict counts most in your life*
*Is the man staring back in the glass.*
*He's the one you must satisfy beyond all the rest,*
*For he's with you right up to the end;*
*And you will have passed your most difficult test*
*When the man in the glass is your friend.*
*You may be the one who got a good break,*
*And think you're a wonderful guy;*
*But the man in the glass says you're only a fake*
*If you can't look him straight in the eye.*
*You may fool the whole world down the pathway of years.*
*And get pats on the back as you pass;*
*But your final reward will be heartaches and tears*
*If you've cheated the man in the glass.*
—*Dale Wimbrow*

*Don't be afraid to express yourself.*
*Make choices that make a difference in your life.*

—Melvin Murphy

## Expressions of Desires

Many people desire the treasures that life has to offer. Following are categories to help you identify your desire. By realizing what category you are in, you will have a better understanding of your character and what you are striving to attain. You can therefore increase your desire in that area and turn that desire into action. The categories are:

- **Desire To Be Free.** Having freedom is your right as a human being. Having freedom is a right many people take for granted until it's taken away. You can lose your freedom by becoming incarcerated for crimes, being confined in a bad marriage or being enclosed in self-doubt in achieving personal success. Having freedom is the opportunity of choice—in other words, how you decide to live your life ethically, morally, right or wrong, successful or not is the choice you have and should always have.

There are various kinds of freedom. The first is *physical freedom*. When the right to come and go has been taken away, there isn't any pleasure in it, such as being jailed for several years or being stranded on an island. The first thought or desire is to get off that island—to be free. Physical freedom is very important. It is priceless and should never be taken for granted—many people have died and are still dying to give this right to others. Remember, you don't know what you have until it's gone. Make choices that make a difference in your life.

The second kind of freedom is *emotional freedom*. Having emotional freedom is being able to express compassion, love, and excitement to others and within ourselves without paying a humiliating price for giving it freely. Emotions can leave lasting impressions. For example, people in corporations who fight their way up the corporate steps and make it to the top are often scarred emotionally. Many people have changed their morals, performed less than ethical behavior despite the consequences, to reach the top—in principle, they had to swim with, be eaten by, or become a shark to survive in the corporate world. This can affect anyone emotionally.

In personal relationships, emotions are a sensitive issue and it is not wise to play with a person's emotional well-being. For instance, men are often accused by women of not showing their feelings and emotions. This may be true in some cases but most men can love as hard and as deep as a women can. Don't play with someone's emotions, even if they do not display their emotions on the surface. Do not gamble with someone's emotions. It will lead to big trouble.

Finally, the last freedom is *psychological freedom*. Having psychological freedom is like having peace of mind. The freedom to learn, experience and discover new things allows people to be individualistic in their thought processes. Being free to think independently is what makes each of us unique.

Freedom is expressed in many forms. We have freedom of choice every day of our free lives. With psychological, physical, and emotional freedom, we are able to understand who we are and by not being afraid to express ourselves through our desires.

• *Desire To Discover.* To discover is to arrive at thorough search or study. When people gain knowledge, they gain a greater sense of self-confidence. Discovery is like putting all of the pieces of a puzzle on the table, identifying and placing the pieces together, and seeing the big picture once the puzzle is complete.

Discovery signifies that something has been found or realized for the first time. To discover that you have the ability to attain your goal or find new routes to an old destination, pass a difficult examination, or prepare a gourmet meal is helpful in confidence building. Do not be afraid to try things—be adventurous.

• *Desire To Create.* Everyone has creativity within them. Creativity is merely having imagination, originality, and ingenuity. It is part of the desire in human existence. To see creativity at its finest hour, watch a child playing with toys, go to an advertising firm and observe how illusions are made, or watch construction workers build a house over a period of time—we are always creating.

To create is to give life or produce into reality. In life, the most divine creation is the creation of human life. In business, nonprofit organizations are always creating ways to have fundraising events. In science, the human mind is the greatest instrument for creation. Let your imagination fly and allow your spirits to soar to greatness.

• *Desire Excellence*. In all that you decide to do, always have the pursuit for excellence. Excellence simply means being or having superiority or expertise in something—in other words be the best at what you do. Many people have said that "practice makes perfect." Before your practice becomes perfect, it must be practiced perfectly every time—so with this new rule, perfect makes perfect. For example, five time gold medalist of the 1994 United States Gymnastics Championship, Dominique Dawes, who made history by reigning as the "most dominating one-time women's national champion," clenched the position of champion by being perfect. "I just went out there to hit my sets" she said, referring to executing her performance to perfection.

All of the practicing paid off for her; but she had to execute each of her routines without flaw, she had to perform perfectly to be perfect, which rewarded her with excellence. So, learn to rehearse perfectly.

• *Desire To Win*. Is winning everything or is it how you play the game? The answer to this question is that, in life—especially in America—no one likes a loser. Everyone wants to be on the winning team or be associated with a winner. Many people desire to triumph in all quests because it brings a certain opulence and self-achievement in life. For example, Dominique Dawes has achieved a certain opulence because she is a winner; she is the second woman to win a clean sweep in the gymnastics Nationals. With this celebrated milestone comes affluence, opulence, and success.

At the same time, isn't it how you play the game that's more important? In life, how the game is played deals with having good morals, principles, and ethics. While having the desire to win, in business, sports or life, always hold yourself to the highest ethical standards because having good morals and ethical standards makes a winner. Finally, in the game of life having the desire to win honorably is how the game is played and won successfully.

When a person has achieved success, what's next? Rarely do we discuss the issue of what happens once a person has reached their goals or the level of success they desire. If you have reached the level of success you desire and feel perplexed about what's next in your career—don't be. Once you have attained the success you want, continue to achieve more success at different levels. For example, upon successful completion of high school, people will go in one of two ways—to further their education in some way or proceed uninterrupted into the world of work.

If a person has chosen to further their education and successfully completes technical school or the first four years of college, that's another level of success from high school. If they chose to continue to the graduate level, on to the postgraduate level and receive their doctorate, that's considered to be a different level of success after achieving the initial level of success. It is wise to continue building on the success you've already gained.

To further explain, utilizing the comparison of relationships, people carry past experiences with relationships and life experiences into their new relationships and new life experiences. When two individuals decide to build a lifelong relationship, they must grow in different levels of the relationship. For instance, when two people meet, that's the first level of success. (It often takes work to find that special someone.) The second level is to get to know each other well enough to make a decision to be in a relationship.

The third and final level is to build and maintain the relationship through a willingness to compromise for the sake of making the other person happy—such as knowing the likes and dislikes of the other person. Once you are at the level of success you seek, remember to continue to build to levels of greater excellence while maintaining what you already have. Additionally, once you have reached your level of success, leave a legacy by helping others reach their level of success.

How does a person maintain success? You can maintain the success you have achieved by continuing to follow the rules that led to your success. For example, when working for an employer, you maintain your responsibilities by following the rules of the position and the company. If you maintain a certain level of attendance, are a team player, have a positive attitude, and are a higher performer, you are rewarded for your workmanship and dedication by receiving commendations, bonuses, and promotions.

Once the promotions are awarded and you rise higher in the organization, you've achieved success. To maintain that success, continue to follow the path that afforded you the success by continuing to perform at a certain level of proficiency.

*THE HUMAN BODY IS A SHRINE...NOT AN AMUSEMENT PARK.*

—*Melvin Murphy*

## STRESS REDUCTION THROUGH SPORTS

Stress is an important concern to people following their dreams. Often, they are making decisions, transitions and altering their lifestyles to find freedom by following their dreams. Having unhealthy levels of stress can impede your progress in achieving your goals. Being able to recognize when you are stressed will help you make the appropriate decisions in your life allowing you to be successful.

As an entrepreneur, your stress will increase because of the enormous responsibilities you hold—building a business, providing the payroll or securing work for employees. At times, you may become cantankerous, short-tempered, pushy, have mood swings, or always seem to be in a pensive state. Stress can affect anyone, any occupation or situation. Consider the following case:

On November 21, 1987, I received a telephone call that would change my life. The call came from a technical manager at IBM Corporation in Washington, D. C. He was calling to inform me that I had been selected to fill a position in their national service division. Then he politely, professionally and enthusiastically extended an offer of employment to me.

While holding the receiver of the phone, my knees buckled, and I immediately sat on the bed. I was filled with happiness and wanted to jump for joy, but I remained calm vocally and emotionally—as if it wasn't a big deal. We continued to talk and set a start date for my employment. The conversation ended and I placed the receiver of the telephone in the phone cradle and then...all of a sudden I became a human grasshopper, jumping and shouting all over the room, jumping on the bed, rolling on the floor, kicking my legs and feet in the air. Sweat began falling, for I was filled with bliss: my years of hard work had finally paid off and I had reached the corporation I had yearned to work for all my adult life.

Next, I began calling my closest friends and family locally and long distance to spread the good news. Everyone I called was as happy for me as I was for myself. After all of the telephone calls had been made, I sat down and began to see visions of myself succeeding and climbing the corporate ladder to where I wanted be.

On December 1, 1987, I started my first day with "big blue" as an engineer student—let me remind you that I did not hold an engineering degree. I later discovered that I had been selected over five other candidates who held engineering degrees. (At the time IBM received about one million applications a year, and they only interviewed and employed the top ten percent.)

Becoming aware of this astounded me. I began to feel special and part of an elite company. On the first day, I figured since IBM was nicknamed "big blue" I would wear a blue shirt to go with that image. That was my first mistake—I was told by one of my new peers (not management) that I was not allowed to wear blue shirts or any shirts with color in them. I was told to wear white shirts only.

I was also told I could not wear tweed jackets or plain slacks. I was informed that I was required to wear matching two or three-piece suits. The unwritten rule of white shirts and dark suits that many have heard about does exist at IBM; some people do buck the system, but their careers don't go anywhere. Needless to say, I purchased many white shirts, and I still wear a few today.

I completed processing and received my badge. I would begin to prepare for my service school located in Chicago, Illinois, in January 1988, where the winter winds will freeze any part of your body that is uncovered—like a piece of ice. I received first-hand experience in the "windy city." It takes a special person to live in Chicago in the winter time, and I'm just not one of them.

Also, I remember our service school hours were from 3 p.m.

to 11 p.m. A group of us would lock arms to walk back to the corporate apartments located on Michigan Avenue—the gold coast. The apartments were not far enough to take a cab, but far enough to feel the cold as we walked. We would lock arms to stay warm and to keep from being knocked down by the stinging wind—anything uncovered, like ears, nose, or face, became frostbitten.

The stress in my life began. I was placed in an office without windows. There was a computer and a desk in the room. This is where I started my in-house training to prepare me for my service school in Chicago. My stay in this room would last for one month, eight hours a day; reading and being tested on a computer—and an old model, at that. However, my job was to learn the material that I had been given.

I completed desk top computer training and was placed in the mainframe group, known as the large system group. This is a group where engineers are placed after they have worked their way up from the small systems group: it's like a reward for doing well over the years. This process should take five to ten years, but I started in that position.

Once I returned from training in Chicago, I was immediately sent in to the field. IBM management expected you to conduct diagnostic procedures as if you had been doing it for years. Management was supposed to assign a seasoned customer engineer—someone who was required to give me field training and show me the ropes. In my case, management just threw me from the frying pan into the fire. This was the first time in my life I had experienced stress of the worse kind.

They didn't assign me a trainer until I began to protest to the technical manager who had extended an offer of employment to me. Unbeknownst to me, while I had been away training for the last six months, the technical manager had acquired another position within the company—it was with EEO (Equal Opportunity Office). My protest did not go over too well with management. I was assigned a field trainer; but this field trainer resented the fact that he was assigned to me and he let me know it, too.

He felt indignant about how I was placed in the large system group. I had no idea that was not where a person was supposed to start in the company. Nevertheless, I was in the group and in my mind I was there to do a job and I was there to stay. This field trainer basically told me that I shouldn't be in the group and IBM should not have hired me. I immediately knew where I stood with him (adding more stress to my life) and I knew he would not provide me with the best field training he could—and although I was told he was one of the best, I never witnessed it and he never showed me anything about the job. In fact, he refused to allow me to assist with anything. I began to evaluate the situation, wondering why this guy, who did not know me or my abilities to excel at this position if properly trained, didn't like me and refused to help me. I was nice and professional at all times, had an eagerness to learn, but I didn't understand his attitude. To this day I still remain in the dark about why he didn't like me. One thing is for sure, they never told us in service school to expect someone to not accept you as a part of the team.

I was eventually reassigned to another field trainer and to his account, which was the FBI Headquarters (Federal Bureau Investigations) in Washington, D. C. This field trainer was willing to train me and he did a good job. Incidentally, this field trainer was the person who told me about the unwritten dress code with the white shirts. After a certain amount of time with this field trainer, he was reassigned and I assumed his account responsibilities at the FBI—my first account.

What does this mean? It essentially meant I was in charge of a small business within a business at the FBI. If the FBI needed anything for computers, they came to me. If the computers needed maintenance, they came to me. If the FBI wanted to install, relocate, or troubleshoot new computers, they came to me. I was the IBM Corporation to the FBI. (Keep in mind that I had to continue training on the terminal in that small office, go away for more training in Chicago and Atlanta, Georgia.) The stress was mounting.

The stress was still mounting when I was assigned three additional accounts. I managed these computer rooms as small businesses. This meant I had to keep the customer, my peers, and my management happy, along with keeping the paperwork, inventory, and response time in order for each site. To add to this, I was required to assist other Customer Engineers on their accounts when they were on vacation or out ill. I was really stressed at this point.

For five years I lived my life under intense pressure, tension, and anxiety. At the age of 29, I began experiencing chest pains because I was under unhealthy levels of stress. I even had a car accident because I was under stress. I do not recall what exactly happened or who was at fault, for my mind was not on driving the car. I was completely unaware of what was going on around me.

As I approached a traffic signal, I saw a green light, and as I passed through the intersection I saw a red light. It was raining and the roads were slippery and a car was suddenly in front of me. I hit my brakes and began to slide and I hit the other car. The car began to spin like the spin cycle in a washing machine; when it finally came to a stop, I pulled along the shoulder of the road. I emerged from my car shaking like I was at the North Pole without a coat, with the rain running down my face. I had just been in my first car accident. I ran over to the other car, and discovered that the woman was unharmed and her car was also fine. She pulled her car onto a side road...then all of a sudden a man came running over shouting, *"I saw the whole thing. I called the police. I'm going to stay here so you don't have any trouble; I'm a police student,"* directing his statements at me. This assured me the accident wasn't my fault. While waiting for the police, I began talking with the woman from the other car. She lived up the street from the accident site, and I lived about six miles from the scene. It was her birthday; she was celebrating and had been drinking alcohol.

Before the police arrived, we agreed to repair our own cars. She had no physical damage to her car and my car had $1500 worth of damage. The police arrived, and an accident report was filed. The policeman made sure no one was injured or needed medical attention. He also made sure each of us had car insurance—we both did. At that point we all departed.

You are probably asking yourself, "why didn't he tell the

police she was drinking and the accident was her fault?" Well, the man who ran up had disappeared; and I didn't want to see this woman get into trouble with the law, but mainly I wasn't 100 percent convinced that it wasn't my fault. I was highly stressed out from my job at IBM and my conscience would not allow me to ruin her life for the sake of getting my car repaired by her insurance company.

The stress had taken its toll on me. While driving home I began telling myself that I could no longer go on like this; I had become physically ill. The company I grew to love was physically and mentally destroying me.

I asked myself, how had I survived this long? The answer was, I survived for five years because of martial arts. I started with IBM on December 1, 1987. I started my martial arts training on January 8, 1988.

This high impact cardiovascular training sustained me and allowed me to remain at IBM for those years. The martial arts training also helped me realize after five years that I needed to take action to rid myself of the stress problem—for the martial arts could not make me immune to the level of stress I was experiencing any longer. I had to make a change for the better, and I did. I quit IBM. I quit IBM and started a company to help others in corporations reduce stress from their lives through sports.

What is stress? Stress is a mentally or emotionally disruptive influence placed upon the body. Our bodies are shrines, not amusement parks. We need time to rest, relax, and recover from disruptive influences like anxiety and distress in our personal and business life.

High levels of stress can reduce a person's ability to perform any task effectively. It can cause chest pains, heavy breathing, stiffness in the neck, shoulders, back and head (temples). Stress can also cause sleepless nights and drain energy.

High levels of stress can cause mental impairment and trigger irritability. Stress can cause memory loss and increased alcohol or drug use. Having high levels of stress can also cause mood swings.

To reduce stress, consult your doctor for advice. If you feel your level of stress can be controlled without a doctor, then find a release through sports. Find a sport that has a cardiovascular workout such as martial arts, running, or boxing. Find a sport that you will remain interested in, and make a commitment to excel in the activity while reducing your stress.

If you are uncertain about your stress condition, take the Body, Mind and Fitness Survey on the following page. Take this survey as openly and honestly as you possibly can. Then follow the directions on the last page. Good luck!

**DESIRE: THE EMOTIONAL APPETITE FOR SUCCESS**
**BODY, MIND AND FITNESS SURVEY**

1. *My capacity to relax in a stressful situation is:*

    A. Excellent

    B. Good

    C. Fair

    D. Poor

2. *I would evaluate my flexibility as:*

    A. Excellent

    B. Good

    C. Fair

    D. Poor

3. *I would evaluate my strength as:*

    A. Excellent

    B. Good

    C. Fair

    D. Poor

4. I would evaluate my coordination as:
    A. Excellent
    B. Good
    C. Fair
    D. Poor

5. In the middle of my work day, my energy level is:
    A. High
    B. Medium
    C. Low

6. In general, my concentration level when under stress is:
    A. Excellent
    B. Good
    C. Fair
    D. Poor

7. I would evaluate my capacity to relate well with others when under stress as:
    A. Excellent
    B. Good
    C. Fair
    D. Poor

8. I would evaluate my self-confidence level as:
    A. Excellent
    B. Good
    C. Fair
    D. Poor

9. *I would evaluate my health as:*
    A. Excellent
    B. Good
    C. Fair
    D. Poor

10. *I would evaluate my creativity when under stress as:*
    A. Excellent
    B. Good
    C. Fair
    D. Poor

11. *I would evaluate my productivity when under stress as:*
    A. Excellent
    B. Good
    C. Fair
    D. Poor

12. *I would evaluate my smoking habits as:*
    A. None
    B. Heavy
    C. Light
    D. Average

13. *I would evaluate my sleeping habits as:*
    A. Excellent
    B. Good
    C. Fair
    D. Poor

14. *I would evaluate my health as:*

    A. Excellent

    B. Good

    C. Fair

    D. Poor

**Scoring:**

If you have circled letter A more than six times, you are in excellent condition. Keep up the good work.

If you have circled letter B more than six times, you are in good condition. Congratulations.

If you have circled letter C more than six times, you are on the borderline. Reevaluate your workout. You can achieve anything.

If you have circled letter D more than two times, you are headed towards trouble. See your doctor and redesign, reevaluate, or start your workout. Remember, take action and make things happen.

*LET'S GO TO THE MOUNTAIN TOP AND LOOK OVER...AND BELIEVE.*

—Melvin Murphy

## A TRIBUTE TO THE GREATNESS OF DR. MARTIN LUTHER KING, JR.

Martin Luther King, Jr. went to the mountain top, looked over and saw the promised land. A land of hope, chance, and certainty for all who believe in the truth. A land made as a peace ground for all men, women, and children. This land is your land; this land is my land. This land is the earth we walk on every day.

At the mountain top, Martin Luther King, Jr. was able to see further than his imagination. He was able to see the joy of a smile, the power of love, and the faith in all people. He was able to envision the inventiveness of harmony through non-violence. He was able to teach that there is strength in unity through integration of people of all nationalities.

He told us that he might not get there with us, but he knew we as a people would get to the promised land. He knew that if we believed in kindness, respect and had ethical values, that we would get to the promised land. He knew that we as a people would have to work together through communication. He knew that we as a people of a great nation would live in harmony.

Martin Luther King, Jr. had a dream that one day people would not be judged by the color of their skin, but by the content of their character. He had a dream that people would learn to consider the qualities and traits by which people are to be valued. His dream would allow people to be valued on their merits, not on the color of their skin.

Martin Luther King, Jr. was a dreamer who believed "justice should roll down like water and righteousness like a mighty stream." He was a man who had a vision of what the world could be like instead of the way it was when hatred and violence were allowed to rise against one type of people.

Dr. King's childhood was important to the man he became. Many journalists, scholars, and members of the public ignored Martin's childhood. Dr. King joined the church at the age of five. He and his siblings Christine and A. D., had no choice but to attend church to hear their father sermonize countless church services and guest preachers. Born on January 15, 1929, as Michael Luther King, Jr., he grew up in Atlanta, Georgia, on Auburn Avenue. From 1935-1944, Michael attended David T. Howard Elementary School, Atlanta University Laboratory School and Booker T. Washington High School.

At the age of eighteen he was licensed to preach and became assistant to his father, who was pastor of Ebenezer Baptist Church. His father, Michael Luther King, Sr., changed his name to Martin, which automatically changed his son's name also.

As a child, Martin Luther King, Jr. lived across the street from his best friends. All were good ball players, but most of all they were good friends, until things began to drastically change.

When Martin started school he hoped that he and his best friends would go to the same school. But you must remember that in 1935 black children were not allowed to attend the same school the white children. Yes, his best friends were white. When the school bus came to pick Martin up, his best friends were not on it, and they were also not at his new school. Nevertheless, Martin was excited about school and couldn't wait until he got home to tell his friends about his first day.

As usual, his friends were playing baseball in the yard. When Martin went to join in his friends suddenly stopped playing and said, "We are not allowed to play with you anymore because you are black and we are white." Martin was very upset. His parents explained what segregation was, but Martin refused to accept this.

He tried to forget what had happened. Then one day his father took him into town to buy some shoes, and a white clerk refused to serve them because they were sitting in the front of the store, which was for whites only. An argument ensued and Martin's father grabbed him and walked out of the store without purchasing the shoes. On another occasion, a policeman pulled over the elder King's car, rudely demanding, "Boy, show me your license." Martin didn't understand why until his father explained once more the details of segregation. At this early age Martin promised to help end segregation.

Between the ages of eleven and twelve, Martin attempted suicide twice, once because of his brother's accidental injury of his grandmother and the other when his grandmother died naturally. After recovering from her death, Martin passed the entrance examination to Morehouse College at the age of fifteen, without graduating from high school. After earning his degree in Sociology from Morehouse College, an all male-institute in Atlanta, Martin Luther King, Jr. went on to the prestigious Crozer Theological Seminary and obtained a Bachelor of Divinity. The civil rights movement delayed his moving to Boston University where he eventually received his Ph.D.

Martin Luther King being thrust into the spotlight began with a lady named Rosa Parks. Many of you may not know that King's unique status was not self-evident to many who breathed the movement, slept the movement, suffered the movement and sometimes died for the movement. King was a minister, but so were many others, including most of his lieutenants. Why was King singled out to be a leader? He mastered Gandhian nonviolence, but so did dozens of others. He volunteered for jail duty, but so did hundreds of others. He headed a major political organization, but so did others like James Farmer, Roy Wilkins, the President of the Brotherhood Railroad Porters Union, John Lewis, and James Forman. He choreographed dramatic confrontations with Southern sheriffs, but so did others like Farmer, Lewis, and Hosea Williams.

Why was King singled out to be a leader? He exhibited statesmanlike abilities to listen, deflect hostile criticism, and lead despite deadly opposition; but so did Farmer, Lewis, Diane Nash, Fannie Lou Hamer, and many other civil rights activists. King proved to be an expert political strategist and organizer, but so did Farmer, Lewis, Nash, Ella Baker, Bayard Rustin and many other civil rights activists. He risked his life, but so did Farmer, Medgar Evers (whose killer was recently convicted), James

Meredith and literally hundreds of others. King survived attempted assassinations, but so did Farmer, Meredith, all of the Freedom Riders, and others. He was martyred for the cause of black rights, but so were Evers, Malcolm X, and many more.

Serving as a minister, practicing nonviolence and dying for the cause are all admirable and uncommon qualities. But none of these qualities alone or in combination made King unique, for he shared them with Farmer and their colleagues. They all believed in one thing, which I hope this poem that I have written will explain:

### IN THE LIGHT OF TODAY

*The snow, The rain, The sun,*
*For classes that remain this day.*
*Tokens of creation given to all.*
*Egyptians who left a rhyton*
*and a stele to be learned and*
*shared by all.*
*On this very day, much*
*blood, civil wars and hatred*
*have overshadowed love and peace.*
*As the snow floats to the cold ground*
*with rain making slush as cement grass*
*forces discontentment, children play,*
*others pray, for a better day.*
*The sun rises in the east*
*which is shared by all*
*don't blink your eyes for night*
*will fall and be shared by all.*
*Don't fear what leers in darkness,*
*you can be my eyes, my friend, my protector*

and watch after my shadow. Guns,
weapons and spies are near, people
unite and there can be no fear.
When the discovery leans toward
the sky, in the twinkle of an eye,
it vanishes in to shy flames, fuel
lagging behind, when that rocket lands
on the moon, it's for a nation, you and I.
Dream! Dreams! They do come true,
but first, you must take action, my
Brother, Sister, African, Hispanic,
Catholic and Jew, smile and I guarantee
it will happen to you.
In the light of today,
Passion, freedom and harmony
should always be at play,
please, please my enemy, don't
go astray, remain with us, in the
light of today.
Fill your mind with knowledge
from my land, share my apple,
my orange, accept my hand and
be my friend.
An olympian stumbles and falls,
a nation desires victory, no need
to worry, victory comes after all
and is shared by all.

—Melvin Murphy

Unlike the other civil rights leaders King became a media magnet and superstar. His crusades in Birmingham and Selma attracted international acclaim, while the media yawned in unison when, during the crusades staged by, Farmer and others. Together, dozens of journalists and the public bestowed on King a spiritually resonant, almost magical name that was not the name on his birth certificate. In the eyes of the press and most of America, King emerged as a uniquely powerful leader. Why was King singled out as a leader? What made him a superstar? The answer to these questions can be stated in a single word: Language. Dr. King's unmatched words and philosophy galvanized African-Americans and changed the minds of moderate and uncommitted Caucasians.

Others could embrace nonviolence, get arrested, and accept martyrdom. But only King could convince middle-of-the-road Caucasians about the meaning of the revolutionary events they were witnessing on their television screens. His persuasiveness did more than surpass that of his colleagues. It enabled him to accomplish what civil rights leaders Frederick Douglass, Sojourner Truth, and W. E. B DuBois, who where King's models and mentors, had failed to achieve. By seeking to persuading Caucasians to accept the principle of racial equality, he made a monumental contribution toward solving the nation's most horrific problem—racial injustice. King began his sermons and speeches by calmly stating this title, and citing his scriptural text. He began slowly, so deliberately he seemed bored. Then he did what he always did when he addressed black listeners: He gradually modulated his rich, baritone voice, picking up speed and emphasis as his hypnotic phrases fell into rolling cadences punctuated by an occasional "Amen" from the audience. Slowly, the baritone voice grew louder and louder until it reached a thunderous roar, when he condemned something. By orchestrating the words of his sermons and speeches with a gospel song, King subordinated (borrowing phrases from others) himself to the religious language sanctified by the Protestant communities.

This was a practice for many years by African preachers. For example, King's speeches, essays, books and magnificent rhetorical triumphs did not reflect his tutelage from his white professors. Nor did his persuasiveness result from his study of any of the great white thinkers such as Plato, Kant, Locke, and Marx, to name a few. King succeeded largely because he resisted numerous ideas proferred by his professors and the Great Thinkers. Instead he drew upon two powerful and popular rhetorical traditions.

The first is veritable of sermons delivered and published by Harry Emerson Fosdick, Hamilton, Bosley, and other prominent white preachers. The second and more significant influence was black folk-pulpit sermons of King's grandfather and father, who were both illiterate folk preachers. There are several reasons for the failure of journalists, biographers, and the public to understand how King's language worked. First, researchers have claimed that Martin failed to acknowledge his borrowing and rarely spoke of preaching traditions, white or black. Secondly, there is unfamiliarity with and difficulty in examining folk style sermons.

Just as providing the means of shaping King's magnificent oratory was black folk pulpit sermons taught at an early age, with the help of many unsung heroes. Heroes like preachers and civil rights leaders L. M. Tobin and William Holmes Borders, who laid the groundwork for the freedom struggle.

Speaking of ground work, how did Martin Luther King become a leader? Remember Rosa Parks, a black woman who refused to give up her seat on the bus because she was tired? Before Martin Luther King even knew of Rosa Parks, she had been bailed out of jail. And when he was introduced to her and was asked to speak on Mrs. Parks' plight, Martin Luther agreed. Parks' trial was brief, the verdict predetermined, and she was fined $10 plus court costs. This, my friends, started the bus boycott that would make U. S. history and have a snowball effect for the civil rights movement.

King negotiated between the universe of black folk culture contained within the sanctuary of Ebenezer Church and the universe of print exemplified by libraries, bookstores, and publishers. Not only was this negotiation important to King, it was absolutely crucial to the triumph of the civil rights movement.

What does all of this really mean? It means the movement has handed many people the right to freedom of choice. It has afforded African-Americans the opportunity to sit anywhere on any public transportation or attend any university. It has allowed me to make friends outside of my race. It has given me the opportunity of freedom, which has been paid for with the blood, sweat, and tears of others who have opened the gateway to justice, equality, and the pursuit of happiness. It means the movement has allowed me to learn to read and write without fear of being beaten for my efforts. We could continue to give many good reasons for what this movement accomplished in our lives.

After the Rosa Parks verdict, her attorney filed an appeal; she did not win her appeal. For this reason, the boycott came and the people were victorious. Because of the victory, on the courthouse steps civil rights activists Ralph Abernathy, E.D. Nixon, and Rev. French discussed with Martin the desirability of forming a permanent organization to help with future problems like the boycott.

Martin agreed, so the Montgomery Improvement Association (MIA) was formed. Who singled Martin Luther King out to be a leader? He didn't jump up and say," I'm going to be the leader." Who singled him out? As Ralph Abernathy's widow, Juanita, said—and I agree with her—"You can't just say that one person did it. There's no such thing. Totally impossible...For Martin Luther King to be the Martin Luther King he was, there had to be a whole lot of little folk, a whole lot of unsung heroes...to give him impetus, to give him the stamina. And they made their contributions. They were just not heard as loudly."

The Montgomery Improvement Association was the brainchild of Ralph Abernathy. Nixon was supposed to choose a president as its leader. A dynamic speaker was required, and guess who possessed this quality? Martin. At the first MIA meeting, Martin Luther King sat back in his chair and heard his name nominated for the presidency by Professor Rufus Lewis. Instantly, the motion was seconded and carried. "The action caught me unawares" he said. "It happened so quickly that I did not even have time to think it through." So later, he discussed it with Coretta and she assured him "whatever you do, you have my backing."

The MIA was victorious in most of its endeavors, and prompted the forming of the Southern Christian Leadership Conference (SCLC). Voting for the SCLC presidency was much like the MIA, but this time the person elected should have no enemies, no ties to the community, and be able to relocate to another area. Guess who was elected? Martin. The first SCLC was formed in Atlanta, where it remains today at the M. L. King Center.

Martin Luther King, Jr.'s style, desire for freedom mixed with life experiences, made him a great leader. But what was the reason for all of his wants and desires for people as a whole? There were many. Let's not forget the real purpose of why Martin Luther was great. He was a man who wanted peace, love, and happiness for our nation. He touched everyone's life directly or indirectly.

I don't know if you have realized this or if you will agree with me, but it's hard to tell who the heroes are today. Some political figures are not doing their jobs; the police are being hired for murder, or drug protection; the movie stars will not speak out on issues without being paid millions of dollars. We have children killing children; we have people trying to destroy the table of brotherhood which has been established so you and I can live in peace and without fear as "one nation under God, indivisible, with liberty and justice for all."

Martin Luther King believed in this principle and I want to call on each of you to help continue to make his dream a reality. We must learn to communicate with others effectively. We as an intellectual nation can change relationships through the art of communication and understanding.

With positive communication, we can calm the hostility that some people may hold against others. With positive communication we will be able to grasp how others perceive a situation or problem. If we communicate with each other, we will learn that people can learn to love.

As Martin Luther King so eloquently said, "There is something that I must say to my people, who stand on the worn threshold which leads in the palace of justice. In the process of gaining our rightful place, we must not be guilty of wrongful deeds. Let us not seek to satisfy our thirst for freedom by drinking from the cup of bitterness and hatred."

"We must forever conduct our struggle on the high plain of dignity and discipline." King went on to say, "For many of our white brothers, as evidenced by their presence here today, have come to realize that their destiny is tied up with our destiny. And they have come to realize that their freedom is inextricably bound to our freedom. We cannot walk alone."

"And as we walk, we must make the pledge that we shall always march ahead. We cannot turn back." For those of you reading this book, whoever you are, wherever you live, with your help we will go to the mountain top and look over and believe. Somehow we will not allow the past to repeat itself, knowing our current situation will change for the better. Let us not wallow in the ravines of despair.

"Let us lift every voice and sing until earth and heaven ring, let it ring with the harmonies of liberty, let it re-sound loud as the rolling seas. Let us sing a song full of the faith that the dark past has taught us, let us face the rising sun of our new day begun, let us march on until victory is won."

As Martin Luther King said: "And when this happens, and when we allow freedom to ring, when we let it ring from every village and every hamlet, from every state and every city, we will be able to speed up that day when all of God's children, black men and white men, Jews and Gentiles, Protestants and Catholics, will be able to join hands and sing in the words of the old Negro spiritual: "Free at last. Free at last. Thank God almighty, we are free at last."

**With my sincere appreciation and thanks to Martin Luther King, Jr. for giving me the freedom to make choices in my life, without fear of retaliation from those who have not made it to the mountaintop to see the promised land.**

—Melvin Murphy

*NECESSITY IS THE MOTHER OF TAKING CHANCES.*

—Mark Twain

## THE EXPRESSION FOR UNITY

What can I do to increase unity?

The barriers of color and racial bias prevail as a problem in America. When considering the effect this problem has upon people in America, it becomes an announcement to the world that America's salad bowl no longer contains a mixed salad. History has allowed us to realize that we still have much work to do to end the raising of new racial bias against people, and in continuing to stamp out the racial problems that remains from past generations.

We must open our eyes and see that America has made exceptional progress in closing the gaps of unity among all people; but we are losing our most powerful weapon to seal the gap, which is love and respect for people. How we decide to control this hazardous emergency will determine the freedom of choice, cultural vitality as a nation, and America's copyrights to how dreams are made and fulfilled. The physique of America today, affords us the indulgence of having a strong nation through unity. The sacrifice this great nation will pay for allowing the past hatred, division of people, and lack of respect to rise or continue is its own annihilation.

We have the knowledge, the capability, and the strength to end this possible destruction. All we are lacking is the desire to take action. Thankfully, we have made substantial strides in securing the gaps in solidarity. There will always be people who refuse to embrace the concept of unity and the wholeness of a nation. The chaos and public outcry against unity, cross-cultural loving, and exterior provocateurs symbolize a strategy of destruction of a goodwill system. There are more problems to be concerned with, such as AIDS, poverty, world and domestic hunger, world peace, economic problems and day to day violence. The chimes of time are ringing more loudly than ever calling people to unite.

The term discord represents mayhem, strife, contention, conflict, disagreement and the like. The term unity represents an order that is permissive; it allows people to join hands in teamwork, camaraderie, family—a strength undivided. Unity is enterprising and is more important than discord.

Unity is an enthusiastic endorsement of lack of strife, conflict, and the arrival of harmonious action for all people. Today unity is a short-range action plan with a long-range goal. We can look around to see the lethal consequences of a community that is weak in unity. It conveys the need of closeness, both physically and psychologically. It gives us a society that's fighting against each other instead of for each other. We can't fight the division of people, hatred, and lack of respect with our fists—we must fight with our hearts.

What are the requirements for unity? We define unity as the condition of being one. A condition of being together. The first requirement for unity is the acceptance of goodwill. Unity has become a demand in America and it is certain to be supplied because we are all connected. We are connected by the work we do, the places we shop, the schools and universities we attend, and the sports we play or watch—we are all connected in some form, and the acceptance of goodwill is merely letting go of a division of the past to help our fellow man and woman in the present.

The American people must become a team or this nation will continue to wreak havoc and see devastation by destroying the remaining bonds of unity. Now is the time when we must make real promises of unity and togetherness. It's time to rise from the television sets and from reading the newspapers to making the news. We are well behind the times. We must lift our nation from the quicksand of "It's not my problem" to stand on the solid rock of "Help thy brothers and sisters" of all nationalities.

The American people must unite as a team, as they do when they see people in distress. When there is a car accident people band together to help the victims involved, regardless of color, religion or beliefs. All that comes to mind is that those are people are hurt and need assistance.

Today America has been in an accident and needs your help to close the gaps to form a stronger defense for unity. We need your help to prepare for tomorrow. The best preparation for tomorrow is to unite today.

The second requirement for unity is having compassion for all people. Let's be patient with each other. Let's educate each other about our cultures and how we came to be; but most importantly, we must learn that we are all here for one purpose and that is to learn to live together.

The third requirement for unity is respect. Having respect for yourself and others is the greatest start to achieving unity. Having respect and being thoughtful can only come from within—and if you have it within yourself, it will be displayed on the surface.

The need to express unity is evident in America. It is visible in every news story. It is evident in any serious conversation about the state of affairs in our community and country. This desire for unity has manifested itself into the fierce urgency of now.

The final requirement for unity is interest. We must become interested not only in ourselves, but also in others—because nothing is interesting if you are not interested. Invest your time in other people.

Why unite? Because it is one of the many things we have remaining in life that doesn't cost money. It's something we as a nation need and can achieve. America can send men to walk on the moon, or build on the depths of the ocean floors, but we can't eliminate the lack of unity among our own people.

At the same time, we must give recognition to the individuals who have set out to unite with other people. They have decided to add permanence in closing the gaps of solidarity. These are people who want to experience other people, cultures, and turn frowns on grim faces into smiles.

These are people who are interested in the person as a whole person. These are people who will accept others on the basis of merit, not because of how much money they make, the kind of house they live in, or the kind of car they drive. These are people who love people because they are people.

The next time you look in or walk by a mirror, ask yourself, "What can I do to increase unity?"

Make

a world of difference

by building

unity

between

all people

-Melvin E. Murphy

> *Can you do it? Can you do it?*
> *...Yes sir!!!*
>
> —Melvin Murphy

## Procrastination is "the enemy"

What is procrastination? Procrastination is the act of deferral, postponement or putting off an activity until a later time. Often the illustrations of procrastination will mean different things to each of us, such as putting off writing thank-you notes, sending birthday cards or even following our dreams. Procrastination can cause any dream, goal or aspiration to go unfulfilled.

Procrastination can afflict anyone at any time. For instance, when you're trying to get up and out of the bed in the mornings, and you keep hitting that snooze button on the alarm clock, it's because you don't really want to get up—that's called procrastination. But eventually you take action and get up to start your day.

Procrastination is a part of life. At some point, each of us will procrastinate in a situation or on an endeavor. We will procrastinate because the situation is uninteresting to us, or we just plain don't want to do the job, or maybe we fear we may not do well on the project. Many people will procrastinate because of fear of failure or fear of success. Whatever the reasons, do not allow procrastination to interfere with your success.

• *Fear of Failure.* Many people procrastinate because they fear failure. Many people fear they will not place their best foot forward in their endeavor or that they can't live up to the expectations of others—essentially becoming their own worst critics. For example, Debbie is a beautiful, smart, young woman, who has met with disappointment and failure in all of her careers. Debbie has become complacent with procrastination. She believes her place is to be miserable, unhappy and unsuccessful because of her past experiences. Procrastination is her enemy.

Debbie rejects the idea of taking the time to stop and think about what she desires from a career and how to achieve it. She's constantly talking herself out of following her dreams, using failure as her future. So, basically she will not allow herself to dream. Also, she uses famous quotes "like I don't know what I want to do," "what can I do?," or "I don't know what I'm good at" to dissuade herself from taking action.

• *Fear of Success.* Do you become uncomfortable when you think of promotion to the next level at your job? Do you change the conversation when the subject of being promoted to upper-level management comes up? It is difficult to understand why someone fears success—but many people do. It is difficult to understand how someone could intentionally undermine their way to success, but many do, by leaving projects uncompleted, or quitting before completion of the project. Others simply feel success has never been and never will be a part of their future.

Many people work hard to be successful in their endeavors until it comes time for the big pay off—then they don't want it, because they feel they may become a target for criticism or be judged too severely by their peers. Many people decide not to move forward because of the responsibilities that would come with the new position. To overcome fear of success, you must first know you have the confidence to succeed. Seek counseling if necessary, or evaluate yourself, read books, talk to others and then decide to take the necessary action to eliminate fear of succeeding.

• **Overcoming Procrastination.** The best way of overcoming procrastination is to seek the advice of qualified medical personnel or by reading books on the subject. Then develop a plan of action to help assist you in overcoming procrastination. Many people may lack abilities in certain areas, such as time management, which could cause their procrastination. Find the areas you are weakest in and develop them. This will afford you the opportunity to enhance your self-esteem in those areas. Do not continue to procrastinate for every minute you waste and forfeit, the longer it will take you to complete your dreams. Do this by setting goals for yourself, start and complete projects, and become proficient in time management, by establishing a support system with qualified people. Don't be afraid to ask for assistance. Once you have taken action to overcome procrastination, it will no longer be your enemy.

*JUST DO IT.*

—NIKE

## Asking the Right Questions.

Can I achieve this? Will I reach my goal? Is it possible to do that? We often ask ourselves many questions like this, because we are trying to justify taking the action that has been started to achieve a desired goal. Asking the right questions can save time and often headaches when in the middle of a business venture. In the advertising industry, which uses competitive strategy, three main questions are continually asked strategy: Should we compete in? What market should we compete? How should we compete? These questions help advertisers develop marketing plans, media campaigns, and segmentation and positioning plans. Advertisers employ these questions to help guide their strategy.

In the broadcast communication industry five main questions are used to help broadcasters cover and complete major stories. Every newspaper in the United States utilizes these questions to write breaking news stories. The five questions are called the five W's: *Who? What? Where? When? and Why?*

Asking the wrong questions isn't necessarily right, but not asking questions can lead to unwanted problems. The message here is to always ask questions. It can only help in the understanding of a situation or in aiding your belief that you can achieve your desired goals.

*HAVE THE POWER OF PATIENCE...AND MAKE THE RIGHT CHOICES.*

—*Melvin Murphy*

## MAKING THE DECISION

Over the years, many people have tried to define the decision-making process. Hundreds of books have been written on the subject of decision-making and it often becomes a battle of trying to decide which books to read.

For these reasons, this book does not contain any detailed discussions on the decision-making process. Instead, I will introduce a tool that can be utilized in helping to understand the reasoning for the choices we make.

I was recently, introduced to The Unattainable Triad. The triad is nothing more than three words, one placed at each point of a triangle. With these three words, you can clarify your reasoning, and see the unexplained effects you have encountered will experience in your decision-making process. The triad, can also be utilized as a decision-making tool. It has become one of the supporting tools in my personal and professional life.

The logic of the unattainable triad is totally in the hands of the person making or calling the shots. This triad can be used in business as well as in your personal life. There can be no misunderstandings or wrong choices—only the choices you make.

The unattainable triad helps us understand why a project did not succeed, why the quality of a production fell under standards, or how much time or money we are willing to dedicate to a project. The unattainable triad's three words are: price, time and quality. In making a decision you are allowed to choose two words. For example, if you need a brochure printed, which two words will benefit you most? Quality and time. These two words were selected because, if you are in a fast-paced business, quality and time are important. That leaves price. This means you want the quality of a good brochure and you may or may not have the time to wait for it. So, you are willing to pay the price (whatever it is) to get it in a timely fashion.

Let's do one more. A college student has a project due and hastens to get it done. Because he failed to complete it when he had the time, it will lack one of the three triad words. Time and money are the words chosen. If the student is concerned with time and money, that leaves quality. The project will lack quality.

**THE UNATTAINABLE TRIAD**

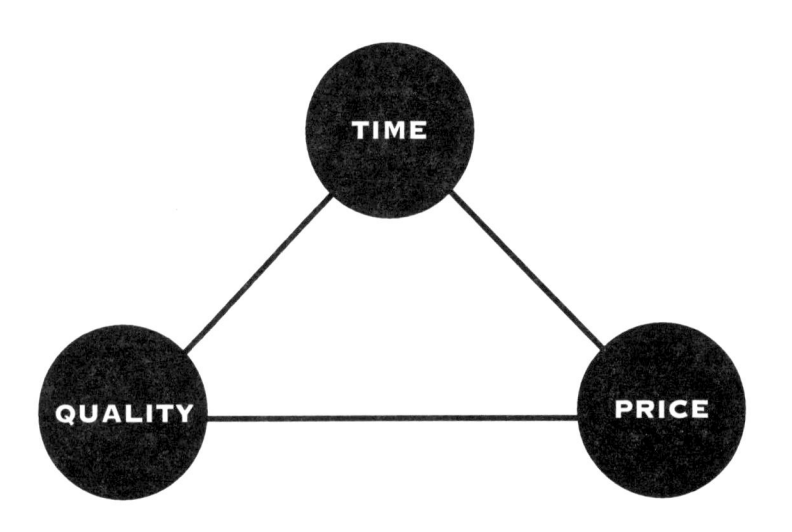

## A Closing Prayer

*The Lord is my shepherd; I shall not want.*

*He maketh me to lie down in green pastures:*

*he leadeth me beside the still waters.*

*He restoreth my soul:*

*he leadeth me in the paths of righteousness*

*for his name's sake.*

*Yea, though I walk through the valley*

*of the shadow of death,*

*I will fear no evil: for thou art with me;*

*thy rod and thy staff they comfort me.*

*thou preparest a table before me*

*in the presence of mine enemies:*

*thou anointest my head with oil;*

*my cup runneth over.*

*Surely goodness and mercy*

*shall follow me all the days of my life:*

*and I will dwell in the house of the Lord for ever.*

—Psalm 23

**ABOUT THE AUTHOR**

Melvin Murphy began his professional speaking career as a way to help bring America closer together and to continue the dream of Martin Luther King, Jr. Now he is the principal in Melvin Murphy Communications, which provides unity keynote speeches and unity training seminars to human rights, and community organizations, associations and corporations worldwide. He is a published poet and the author of a column The Motivational Moment, and the creator of the Progress 2000 a national youth motivation program. In addition, he performs a re-dramatization of Dr. Martin Luther King's speech "I Have A Dream" throughout the year. He has been featured in *Forbes FYI* and *Employee Health and Fitness* magazines and several newspapers, television and radio news broadcasts, including Bloomberg Financial Market Commodities radio news.

Mr. Murphy is known to his friends and business associates as a "catalyst for unity." Melvin's message is that people in America must focus on being Americans and build understanding between all cultures. He enjoys reading, martial arts, talking with people, and a variety of sports, the latest being scuba diving. Melvin Murphy was educated at The American University in Public Communications with a concentration in Advertising. His second major was Sociology. Melvin resides in Fairfax, Virginia.

Bring **Desire: The Emotional Appetite For Success**, to your organization in keynotes speeches and unity training seminars.

Melvin Murphy is available to make a keynote presentations at your next convention, conference or event. For more information call Melvin at **1-800-337-4730**

To contact the author, write:
**Melvin Murphy**
P. O. Box 2868
**Merrifield, Virginia 22116**

**ORDER FORM**

Give the gift of inspiration and motivation to colleagues and friends.

-------------------------------------------------------------

YES! I want ____ copies of *Desire: The Emotional Appetite For Success* at $12.95 each, plus $4.50 shipping and handling per book (In Canada $16.95 in U.S. funds) ISBN 0-9646799-0-6.

*Call 1-800-337-4730 to order by telephone or fax to (202) 331-1622.*

❏ Check enclosed

❏ Charge my account:

❏ Master Card ❏ American Express ❏ Visa

Account # _____ - _____ - _____ - _____

Signature _____
*(required for all charges)*

Name _____

Phone (_____) _____

Address _____

City/State/Zip _____

<br>

Please make check payable to:
*Melvin Murphy*
P. O. Box 2868
Merrifield, Virginia 22116